FIRST FIGHTER ACE

FIRST FIGHTER ACE

In the Cockpit with a World War II Fighter Pilot

STANISŁAW SKALSKI

Translated by John Bednarz, Jr.

Stackpole Books

Guilford, Connecticut

Published by Stackpole Books
An imprint of Globe Pequot
Trade Division of The Rowman & Littlefield Publishing Group, Inc.
4501 Forbes Boulevard, Suite 200, Lanham, Maryland, 20706

Distributed by NATIONAL BOOK NETWORK

British Library Cataloguing in Publication Information available

Library of Congress Cataloging-in-Publication Data
Names: Skalski, Stanisław, author. | Bednarz, John, translator.
Title: First fighter ace : in the cockpit with a World War II fighter pilot /
    Stanisław Skalski ; translated by John Bednarz, Jr.
Other titles: Czarne krzyże nad Polska. English | In the cockpit with a
    World War II fighter pilot
Description: Guilford, CT : Stackpole Books, [2017]
Identifiers: LCCN 2017010139 (print) | LCCN 2017010550 (ebook) | ISBN
    9780811718493 (pbk.) | ISBN 9780811765886
Subjects: LCSH: Skalski, Stanisław. | Fighter pilots—Poland—Biography. |
    World War, 1939-1945—Aerial operations, Polish. | World War,
    1939-1945—Aerial operations, German.
Classification: LCC D792.P6 S5513 2017 (print) | LCC D792.P6 (ebook) | DDC
    940.54/49438092 [B]—dc23
LC record available at https://lccn.loc.gov/2017010139

♾™ The paper used in this publication meets the minimum requirements of American National
Standard for Information Sciences—Permanence of Paper for Printed Library Materials, ANSI/
NISO Z39.48-1992.

Printed in the United States of America

*To my friends and colleagues
who died the lonely death
of a fighter pilot, and whose
graves no mother's hand will tend,
I dedicate this memoir.*

Contents

Preface

I FOUND MYSELF AMONG THOSE WHO IN 1939, THE YEAR IN WHICH THE war broke out, had to face the Luftwaffe. Those first September days showed us how unequal a struggle it would be as our worst fears were confirmed by a tragic course of events.

At the time, the Luftwaffe was unquestionably the most powerful air force in the world. The forces it used against us were at least eight times as great as ours in number alone. But this was not its greatest advantage. Its decisive advantage lay in the quality of its equipment. We had to fight in obsolescent equipment with only negligible combat value. As fighter pilots we flew in planes that were only half as fast and half as armed as our German counterparts. The speed of the Messerschmitt-109 was more than 200 km/hr faster than any of our "Jedenastkas"[1] In this light we Polish fighter pilots in September 1939 found ourselves in a situation analogous to someone running after a speeding car. In fact, our fighter planes were even slower than the enemy bombers they had to pursue.

Under such circumstances the results of air combat were already decided in advance. But we tried not to think about this. Instead, we fixed our attention on the struggle, despite our decided disadvantage.

---

[1] The front-line fighter plane of the Polish air force, the PZL-11C. "Jedenaście" is the Polish word for the number "11" and forms the basis for the plane's nickname. It was the 11th plane in the series that included the PZL-7 fighter plane, the PZL-23 reconnaissance bomber, and the PZL-37 medium bomber. These planes made up the entirety of the combat aircraft at the disposal of the Polish military in September 1939.

These were dreadful, cruel days. For us pilots the hardest thing to accept was that our countrymen, our brothers and sisters, looked up to their own skies in fear, skies that from the very first day were increasingly darkened by the ominous black crosses of the Luftwaffe. Every day thousands of planes appeared from three directions, bringing destruction with them.

What could we, a handful of pilots, do to stem this flood? Faced with a hopeless situation we could not allow ourselves to retreat. So we joined the fight, although not without apprehension. But we did not charge the enemy out of desperation, in obedience to command, as did the cavalry at Somosierra in November 1808. Such tactics offered nothing, because the laws of air combat are different.

Today it is hard to recapture the feeling, but we displayed a moral courage that might be called a feeling of honor, a spirit of pride in ourselves, which was instilled in us in the years before the war. This feeling prevented us from retreating before the enemy. At the same time, in the struggle with this—at the time, undefeated—Goliath we were mindful to live to fight another day. The fear of death causes many people to make mistakes, to produce unintended results. We could not allow ourselves to make mistakes, although we had to make split-second decisions. Normal human fear was overcome by a feeling of one's own responsibility to his country.

I hope this book will help readers understand what it was like to be a Polish fighter pilot—on the ground and in the air—in the uncertain time at the dawn of World War II. So it includes not only the extraordinary events of air combat, but also the more boring events that we experienced on the ground because these events are also important for the reader to gain a full understanding of what we went through. They sometime set the tone. In either case, though, we fighter pilots still faced death at every turn.

CHAPTER ONE

The Enemy Appears

OMINOUS CLOUDS HAD BEEN APPROACHING THE POLISH BORDERS FROM the west for several months as Nazi Germany extended its boundaries and increased its power with easy conquests. Hardly half a year had passed since Munich and the occupation of the Sudetenland when Germany seized another country: German armed forces overran Czechoslovakia. These new and valuable acquisitions only helped to fuel a German war machine that was already working with unparalleled momentum. The echo of these events had hardly subsided when Hitler announced his plans regarding Poland. Before long, he occupied Kłajpeda [Memel], and the threat of attack on us appeared real. The only question was when; the conciliatory commentaries appearing in the press did not deceive us.

At this time there was a partial mobilization in Poland, and border detachments were placed on a war footing. All units of the 4th Air Regiment were moved as far north as possible and were put on alert. Planes were partially armed, with three of the fighter groups making the signal flight.

In northern Poland spring usually comes earlier than elsewhere in the country. This year the warm breezes from the sea had already dried out the ground after the winter snowfalls, and the soft airfields quickly returned to form. The entire squadron was brought up to readiness, and intensive flight activity was undertaken to make up for the shortcomings that resulted from an unpredictable fall and a harsh, snowy winter. Beginning in early March flights of deadly fighters, graceful bombers, reconnaissance planes, and trainers could be seen everywhere in the skies.

Flying activity increased, and life pulsated with the vibrant rhythm of spring.

In a camouflaged tent at the end of the airfield, the signal-flight commander set up his outpost. Equipped with telephones, a radio station, and maps, it was staffed from dawn to dusk.

German reconnaissance flights began to fly freely over future areas of operation. And repeated violations of Polish airspace produced constant alarms and pursuits of the swift, elusive foe.

One day there was a particularly dense drizzle, with dark clouds overhanging the ground, and a low-lying mist shrouding the horizon, limiting visibility to a few thousand meters. I was sitting in the tent passing the time talking with Jan Czapiewski, who was in command of the station. Every now and again the phone would ring and he would pick it up and listen to the news, only to replace the receiver in disappointment.

"Anything interesting?" I asked him.

"No, not really. Either they're testing the line or it's just boring instructions."

"Why don't you pick up some music on the radio?" I suggested.

"No use, the weather's bad, and all you'll get is annoying static."

So he offered me a cigarette.

Just as I began to smoke, the phone began to ring.

"Which one is it?"

"The one on the left," I said as I pointed.

Hardly had he raised the receiver to his ear when his complexion changed dramatically. In a subdued voice he said, "To your planes!"

In no time the tent emptied. Each man ran to his plane: Corporal Klein, Łysek, and I.

A short time later, while we were sitting in our cockpits, with the engines warming up, Jan showed up too. Trying to talk over the sound of the engines he said quickly: "A twin-engined German plane is circling around the region of Bydgoszcz [Bromberg] and is buzzing its airfield."

I pushed my throttle forward, sped out onto the open field, and up into the air. Once in the air I circled to allow the others to form up, and then we were off in the direction of Bydgoszcz. Flying at treetop level I couldn't see much. Terrible atmospheric conditions, a low ceiling with rain and limited visibility, made intercepting the enemy planes a long shot. It was only around Bydgoszcz that the weather improved and the rain completely stopped. We circled its airfield but didn't see anything, so we flew off in a northeasterly direction.

The ground seemed to be sleepy, shrouded in mist, with smoke wafting from the chimneys of farmsteads as I radioed my comrades and asked them if they could see anything. But both replied negatively.

So we returned to the airfield at Bydgoszcz. After we landed the commander of the liaison squadron, which had been stationed at Bydgoszcz for a couple of days as a separate unit, arrived to obtain information about the German plane.

Lieutenant Colonel Rudkowski wasn't able to help me much though. "I was involved with a twin-engined German plane around here," he said. "But after about a half an hour he took off in the direction of Grudziądz [Graudenz]."

I thanked him and took off again in a northeasterly direction.

"He probably came from Prussia about half an hour ago," I thought to myself. "He must be back home by now, in Malbork [Marienburg] or some other airfield, and I'm searching for him like a drunk in a fog."

After a fruitless search in the region of Bydgoszcz and its vicinity, I returned to base.

"So what happened?" asked Janek Czapiewski as soon as I got back to the tent.

"Nothing, as usual! So I flew around for a while. We'll never catch any Germans this way!"

"Yeah," he replied. "We need faster planes, an efficient observational and reporting organization, and good radio communications in order to guide our planes to rendezvous points. But all we ever hear is: It's coming, it's coming—but always too late. And when we ask our pilots if they've seen an enemy plane, the answer is always the same: Yes sir, I saw one flying around earlier, but we couldn't catch up with him." There was an irony in Janek's words.

This was just another example of a brief, typical report describing another futile flight over Pomerania in pursuit of enemy planes. In their modern, faster planes the enemy was able to fly with impunity. Of course, these reports reached Warsaw, but Warsaw never replied, having no effective means of fixing the situation.

The Germans, in the meantime, conducted photographic and visual reconnaissance deep into our northeast sector. Our construction of fortified positions along the Prussian border, begun in the spring, was under constant observation from the air by the enemy.

A second group of pilots arrived to relieve us at dinnertime, after which I dropped by the armorers to make sure that they would have everything ready for the next day's target practice. The chief armaments mechanic told me, "We've got heaps of ammo and aerial targets. There'll be two tow-planes."

So I told him: "Tomorrow, if the weather improves, we'll start practice at seven in the morning," after which I returned to my post, and the monotonous, overcast day slowly slipped away. Only the telephone broke up the boredom with its unnerving ringing.

The weather did improve the next day, and our commander gave the order to begin target practice. As is customary in such cases, the necessary equipment was brought outside. A schedule for target practice was posted for each pilot, and both squadrons were to take part.

"When do you go?" asked Marian Pisarek, who was my closest rival, "I don't see your name on the list."

"I'll wait until you go," I answered.

"Well, I'll show you how it's done, because you've gotten a little too sure of yourself lately," he said.

"We'll see! Maybe you'll beat me, maybe you won't. But do you want to know a secret?"

"What?" asked Marian.

"I adjusted the sights on my guns to a much closer range. And I think that if everything goes well I'll be able to bring something back from the hunt."

"How close did you adjust your sights?"

"Eighty meters."

"Don't you think that that's a little too close?"

"No, in fact I think it might be even a little too far?"

"Now are you so sure of yourself?" I asked him. "I tell you what. Before the actual test let's have a trial shoot. I have a little extra ammo."

"You're trying to trick me," Marian exclaimed.

"Wouldn't you do the same if you were the gunnery officer and it was your job to decide what to do with the extra ammunition?" I asked.

Marian smiled and acknowledged that I was right.

"Okay, then follow right after me. The planes are ready," he said and began to put on his flight suit.

"Wait, I'll go with you," I suggested.

"You want to teach me a lesson?"

"If you can hit the target once, I'll eat my hat," I joked.

"Get outta here!" replied Marian with some irritation.

"Would you hand me my strap?"

When his engine started I had to jump away from the plane because Marian suddenly pulled away.

Each squadron controlled its own target, which encouraged the pilots to try to achieve the best results. Captain Rolski, Captain Leśniewski, Lieutenant Pisarek, Lieutenant Urban, and Corporal Mielczyński were my closest rivals. With each attempt the score changed, and I had to try very hard not to fall behind. Marian was hot on my heels.

A half-hour later, after the first attempts, I was able to examine Marian's target. It showed exceptional marksmanship.

"Did you get a load of my shooting?!" he proclaimed with satisfaction. "If you score half as well I'll buy you a drink."

"Yeah, you did a great job . . . the target is full of holes."

In order not to make a fool of myself, I decided to go first.

After I buckled my strap, Marian didn't miss the chance to cast a few sarcastic remarks in my direction. On this flight I had only half the usual amount of ammunition.

After my first attempt I returned to base, impatiently waiting to see the results.

"How'd it go, deadeye?" Marian taunted. I shrugged my shoulders.

The tow-plane released its targets and they fell to the ground.

"Are they red ones?!" I asked the mechanic.

"Yeah, there're a few of them."

After counting the bullet holes, Marian's face dropped. He stopped taunting me, and impatiently started to inquire how I did.

I jumped back into my plane, and about ten minutes later I was above the target, approaching the tow-plane that was drawing the target.

Attacking from the front and above, I pulled back on the throttle a little and went into a shallow dive. I trained my sights on the tow-plane, moving them slowly toward the target so that I would maintain a straight line of fire. The target began to grow in my sights, and at the instant when it seemed large enough I pulled the trigger. I heard the clatter of my machine guns, stifled by the drone of the engine, and kept on firing until I was out of ammunition. At the last moment I pulled back sharply on the joystick to avoid hitting the target, but it was already too late. My plane dipped and I felt a sharp jolt. Before I even realized it, I was crouching in the cockpit. Out of the corner of my eye I could see the inflated target, which had struck the left side of the fuselage of my plane with its steel ring. When it struck, the plane shook and plunged into a spin.

In an instant I undid my straps and was ready to bail out. My altimeter read 700 meters, so I still had plenty of time. I leveled out the controls, and using the throttle I tried to pull my plane out of the spin. The plane obeyed the controls, but a strange vibration surged through the fuselage. Still, the plane leveled off nicely.

The vibration must not have been anything important . . .

"What was that?" I thought with some trepidation, as I gained altitude.

And the more altitude I gained, the more vibrations I felt. I turned around and looked at my tail. The left stabilizer didn't seem right— twisted and almost loose—it was vibrating a lot. I was seized again by the idea of bailing out. Not knowing the extent of the damage, I expected that at any moment my tail might rip off. And then it wouldn't be easy to bail out. It was hard to make a decision under these circumstances.

"You're shaking like jelly," I thought to myself, trying to cheer myself up.

I climbed to 800 meters and began to try out different speeds to check the possibility of landing.

I pulled back on the throttle and lost speed. The needle on my airspeed indicator fell: 180 . . . 170 . . . 160 . . . 150 . . . suddenly the plane flipped over and began to spin out of control again. After three attempts I finally realized that the plane had to maintain an airspeed of at least 160 km/hr in order to land. "I might overrun the runway, however, if I land at this speed," I thought to myself.

But I decided to try to save the plane and, unbuckling my belts in order to be able to bail out at any moment, I turned my plane in the direction of the airfield. Slowly I descended, not for a moment forgetting about my airspeed. But my approach from over the town complicated the landing a little. So I made a wide turn, a so-called grand tour, and— keeping the plane steady—I reached the edge of the airfield at a speed of 160 km/hr.

I pushed down on the stick until the wheels hit the ground with a thud and immediately shut off my engine. I rolled on for a couple hundred meters more with my tail in the air. Only after I slowed down did the tail finally come down. Then I began to kick the rudder control furiously to brake the plane because I couldn't use the brakes. I tried to steer the plane to the farthest corner of the runway. But even this seemed to be too close. I ended up in the rough terrain that was covered with molehills and shrubs beyond the runway where the plane came to a stop in the mud, and I finally felt relieved.

I restarted the engine to taxi the plane to the hangar, where Marian smiled and clapped me on the shoulders.

"You see, by extending this black line on your plane a little you can get a black cross like the insignia on German planes."

All the rivets and screws that held my plane together were broken off. Only a miracle held the tail in place. In addition, the steel ring of the target mangled the entire left side of my fuselage. The stabilizer was severely damaged too.

Captain Laskowski, the squadron commander, came by. He calmly listened to my report and then examined the plane. After the examination he blew up at me. To my surprise he wasn't angry at me for crashing, but for landing in such a damaged plane.

"In such situations you are ordered to bail out," he shouted.

"But Captain sir," I replied, "I wanted to save the plane. That's why I didn't bail out, and . . ."

"Save the plane! The most important thing is to save yourself, not this old heap! At any moment you could have disintegrated in midair. If that happened in flight there wouldn't be anything left of you or your plane. And then it would have been too late to bail out!"

"Save the plane!" I could hear him exclaim in exasperation as he walked away.

"Listen, I don't want to upset you, but you still might have some trouble, because they might ask you to pay for the repairs," added Mirek Leśniewski. "Better that this is taken care of here, and not sent out to be fixed. Because it'll be an entirely different matter if they have to send it to Warsaw. That'll only mean trouble."

I turned to the chief mechanic and asked, "Chief, what do you think you can do?"

He just gestured with his arms as if to say, "What do I know?"

"Too bad!" I replied.

Then Captain Laskowski returned and told me, "Lieutenant, please be ready to report to the group commander tomorrow at noon." And a moment later he added, "Well . . . all's well that ends well. I'm glad that you were able to get out of this . . . I hope you'll be just as lucky with the group commander."

"Captain, sir!" asked Mirek, "maybe it would be a good idea to find the target for tomorrow's report?! Because if it has a large tear in it it would be a good argument in Skalski's defense."

"That's not a bad idea," he smiled. "But can it be found?"

"Skalski said that he saw where it fell, and maybe we can find it there. I'll take some people, and we'll go looking for it. . . ."

An hour later I was scurrying about the firing range in a truck. We spent a long time looking along its paths and wooded areas. After "landing" in ditches a couple of times, muddied and frozen, we finally found the target. Torn to bits and pocked with bullet holes, it might actually help in my defense.

Night had fallen before we returned from the firing range, heading toward Toruń.

The next day at noon, in regulation uniform, and with the target under my arm, I reported to the office of the group adjutant. The commander came out of his office and, after the necessary formalities, Colonel Stachoń listened solemnly but sensitively to my description of the accident.

"Colonel sir, the target, which I found on the firing range and have left here with the adjutant, clearly shows the effectiveness of firing from close range."

"Please show me," he instructed.

An excellent flier and former fighter pilot, he examined the distribution of the hits, especially in the first ring. His expression reflected his satisfaction.

"From what distance did you fire?"

At this point I tried to use all my powers of persuasion, trying to fix the colonel's attention on my story of the attack, and I tried to change the subject whenever possible so as to lessen my responsibility for the accident. I knew some unknown punishment hung over me because I should have tried to save myself. Nonetheless, I noticed that the commander listened carefully to my explanations.

"Splendid result!" he exclaimed after a little while. "Only the second attack was unsuccessful . . ."

"I missed by . . . a couple of millimeters . . ."

I immediately realized that by returning to the accident I had unnecessarily returned to a sore subject.

"That's good enough for me!" he exclaimed. "You just have to keep a respectable distance, meters, then you'll be safe. Last year, under similar circumstances, we lost one of our junior officers, a very good and experienced pilot. Better to deliver a few less hits than to endanger your life or the plane. You have to learn to resist the temptation to get too close and cross the line of safety."

I waited now for the final decision.

"Since I have not found you to be insubordinate and undisciplined in the performance of your duties, on the contrary, I see that you possess the desire to attain the greatest proficiency in marksmanship, as well as the presence of mind to save your machine, I have decided not to punish you, but I ask you to heed what I as well as your squadron commander have told you. Thank you, you are dismissed."

"Yes sir!" I quickly grabbed the target and skipped out of the office as fast as I could.

"You're lucky that we have a group commander like that, another commander would have settled things differently," said Mirek when I told him about the meeting.

"He's a good pilot and a nice guy!" added Władek Urban. "If you had to answer to some old fart, he would have reamed your ass."

Shortly thereafter the weather improved and spring blossomed in all its charm. The sky cleared and the sun began to warm up.

The squadron, which maintained itself on alert from dawn to dusk, continued to practice constantly. The intensity of our practice air "battles" increased as never before. In groups of different sizes, sometimes deliberately unequal, our fighters practiced combat in precise, agile formations against the background of the azure sky. The 141st (enemy) Squadron painted its tail surfaces lime green, to make it easier to tell the difference between friendly and "enemy" forces.

At the same time lectures on German tactics, which familiarized us with their equipment, enabled us to go into the details of possible future battles. No one doubted that war would come.

German fighter units employed a close order "attack from above." Ours was different: flights of three planes in V formation attacking upwards, starting from the lead formation. And within the flight each plane flew at a different altitude and distance, guaranteeing freedom of movement and observation.

To avoid confusion and the danger of collision, each pilot taking part in these drills matched up with an opponent in the same position in the opposite flight. In this arrangement the flight commanders created one focus of combat, and their wingmen matched up with the wingmen of the opposite commander. Whenever a pilot scored a quick victory, he was required to help out the others. The loser had to give way to the victor and resume combat from an unfavorable position of self-defense.

We flew in a northerly direction. Our "adversary" in one of the opposing flights arrived from the direction of Bydgoszcz.

I was part of the squadron commander's flight, which included Corporal Wieprzkowicz. We had already arrived at the northern end of the airfield when the dark silhouettes of the "enemy" planes appeared in a formation resembling a line of geese.

We approached each other at full speed in head-on attacks. The planes steadily grew larger until I could see that they had white tails. A few seconds later we broke up into what seemed like a cauldron of individual dogfights. After a few turns I started to gain an advantage and was able to creep up on my adversary from behind. He then performed a sudden loop, shifting the fight from a horizontal to a vertical one. After a few loops and turns I got even closer to him, and in a better position to fire. Leszek, seeing the desperate situation, tried to flee by diving to ground level. I pulled up and, seeing my commander in trouble, attacked Marian who already had a kill. I approached from the proper distance, dodged him in time, and returned to combat with a new adversary. Enjoying a great advantage in speed, I pulled my plane up after making a tight turn in front of Marian. At this time Mirek, having no one on his tail, joined the attack and we forced the twisting, turning Marian to surrender. I rolled my Jedenastka over and dove for the ground.

Only three planes now remained above us. I could see the "white" planes glisten as they flew low against the black background of the forest in a V. We broke up to look for targets of opportunity. But this time the "enemy" reappeared with an extra plane.

When we closed again, the fourth pilot, free of the initial phase of combat, hovered over us waiting to see how the dogfights would turn out in order to attack at the right moment and help any of his comrades in critical situations.

I had hardly gotten on a white's tail when I had a plane diving on me. I broke off combat to avoid the attack. But Leszek used this pause and, from his advantageous position, tightened the circle even more. Both planes held tight to my tail. Every moment my position grew worse. I made a loop to break away, trying to lose them in a dive. After performing an extended chandelle,[1] I suddenly cut the throttle hoping to force my attackers to shoot by me if they didn't realize my trick right away. If the trick succeeded I would be on their tail. Unfortunately, only one, the closest plane, shot by me. The other, however, hung tenaciously on my tail. Without losing speed I performed a leisurely turn passing alongside the still-climbing Jedenastka . The other pilot performed the same maneuver following right behind me. Nothing remained for me to do except to dive for the ground. I had lost.

I looked around. Two planes, one of which I recognized to be friendly, were circling low over the forest. This time only "white" planes were above me.

Their wheels delicately skimmed the grass, and the planes touched ground in a tight V formation. Still excited by the exercise, we immediately began a heated discussion on landing. These discussions soon transformed themselves into altercations.

Captain Leśniewski, however, broke them up, calling our attention to the debriefing to discuss the drill.

During the first days of May, I flew a Fokker with a group of other officers at a demonstration in Poznań [Posen]. During the visit loudspeakers broadcast the speech of Foreign Minister Beck. Shortly after the seizure of Kłajpeda, Hitler concluded—on March 23—an economic treaty with Romania, which immediately became another source of raw materials for the Third Reich. Now his intentions toward Poland became clear: unconditional submission, or war.

Then on the 28th of April Hitler revoked the Polish-German non-aggression treaty that had been signed on January 26, 1934.

A week later the Polish Foreign Ministry presented its answer. Poland would not submit to German threats. Colonel Beck expressed the will of the nation, although this became increasingly difficult—with a decisive no!

---

[1] Translator's note: A *chandelle* is an aircraft control maneuver in which a plane combines an ascent with a 180-degree turn at the same time.

Public radios also broadcast the hitherto unexpressed but ardent support of the entire nation.

I could see the uneasiness displayed in the faces of the other pilots. Everywhere I could hear discussions concerning the recent events. The older pilots seemed to sense the danger more acutely. The younger ones, however, seemed to have more confidence in themselves and faith in the fighting spirit of the Polish soldier.

While the mechanics pulled the planes out of the hangars, and the armorers began to arm the guns, the commander called us together.

"We'll practice attacking the camp," he began. "Above all, I would like to instruct the younger pilots who have not had experience in this kind of attack. I leave it to the older pilots to carry out their attacks as they wish. There are different methods of attack in this case, and opinions are divided. But any method that provides good results is good. Nonetheless, it is a difficult task and the achievement of successful results presents real problems. Most of the time the results are zero. I'll take off first, while the targets are being prepared. . . ."

I felt a bit confused by the squadron commander's remarks. But Marian, self-confident as ever, teased me because he hadn't yet shown me his method. I had decided to go with the final flight so as to be able to watch how the other, more experienced pilots attacked.

The exercise took place on the firing range adjacent to the airfield. Scoring was high, so that every hit counted very highly.

"When do you go?" asked Marian coyly.

"Last—but especially after you," I replied.

"You're tricky, you want to watch everyone else. It won't help . . ."

"If there's something you can't do, then it makes sense to watch those who can do it successfully. Above all, I want to watch your attack and its results because I have confidence in you, dammit . . ."

"They're calling for you, lieutenant," the armorer announced. "They say you can begin, everything's ready."

"Tell the squadron commander he can go," I replied, and at once we could see how the older pilots set about their work.

Captain Laskowski took off and disappeared from view in a low-level flight. We waited. From a distance we could hear the sound of his engine, which quickly grew in force. Suddenly a Jedenastka appeared before us, as if glued to the ground. It flew toward us avoiding all low-lying obstacles.

At a distance of about 500 meters, he shot up in a chandelle to gain altitude for a dive. At first we could see the white puffs of machine-gun fire, and then a moment later we could hear the sound of his guns. He then repeated his attack, but this time without firing his guns.

I waited by the phone for the results of the attack and the orders for the second plane to take off.

"Hello, any hits?"

"No," said the voice on the other end of the line. "Tell the second plane to take off."

"This is really not good. I didn't think that the old fox would come up empty," I said in amazement.

Marian didn't say anything in response. Each plane, one after the other, took off and attacked in almost the same manner. And the telephone reported the same result—zero. Finally Corporal Śmiegielski broke the string of bad luck. He even scored highly. Captain Leśniewski did well too, by using a somewhat different mode of attack.

Now it was Marian's turn.

"And don't forget," I yelled to him, "that you are allowed only one attack. Make sure that you don't waste your ammunition."

The look he gave me indicated that he didn't appreciate my remarks. I intently watched as he flew by. His attack was completely different from the others—a dive from high altitude. He finished off his attack with a few bursts from low level, then pulled his plane out of its dive, and took off on a low-level flight over the firing range.

I hung by the phone so that I could get the news of the results as soon as possible.

"Hello, hello, who was that?" asked the voice in the receiver.

"Lieutenant Pisarek!"

"Great results!" I heard the voice say.

"You ought to use his method," I thought to myself.

Marian strutted around like a peacock, proud of his performance.

"How you doing, Stasiu?" he asked.

"Just tell me from what distance, more or less, you fired?" I asked.

"I'll be glad to tell you because I know it interests you so much . . . Approach your target from an altitude of 800 meters and then roll your plane over when you see the targets directly below you. At first you won't see them very well. But try to line one up in your sights anyway. As you descend try to concentrate on their arrangement. Open fire when you get as close to them as possible, moving from one target to the next. Only make sure that you don't fly into the ground. That's all there is to it."

Then he warmly clapped me on the shoulders.

I took my friend's advice to heart. I approached the targets from an altitude of 800 meters, but couldn't find any of them below. Everything seemed to blend into one big yellow-greenish blotch on the ground. It was only when I was in my dive that I detected the outlines of the targets, and finally caught the first column in my sights. The controls became stiff as the plane picked up speed. My altitude decreased rapidly, and the targets became more distinct. My altimeter read 200 meters but I knew that I was already lower than that. It must be slow.

I waited a moment longer.

A short burst at the first column, followed by a slight shift of the stick and my sights were on the next target. I pressed the trigger and the plane shook violently. A dark cloud enveloped my eyes, and it felt as if some powerful force jammed my entire body into my seat. The G force shot the plane upward. In a reclining position I looked at the azure sky for a while.

"Are you nuts?" Marian greeted me as I climbed out of my plane. "Look at the landing gear! Clean them up before anybody notices. It looks as if you crashed into the ground. Ah, the hell with you!"

Marian complained as I cleaned up the landing gear with a branch I had broken off of a nearby shrub. Luckily the landing gear weren't damaged.

"I like this method of attack, Marian. Too bad, I was only able to use up half of my ammunition. I was too low when I began shooting and I ultimately didn't have enough room."

"Pull yourself together!" he said. "After the exercise is over let's all go together to the mess for dinner."

At dinner I asked him, "Marian, how do you think we would do if Hitler decides to attack?"

"Since I only know a little it might be better if I didn't say anything about this matter," he answered after some reflection. "In any event, things wouldn't be very pleasant in the air. But you already know this. How many times have we pursued the Germans and not been able to overtake them or reach their altitude? They play games with us, and do whatever they want. They know only too well that our planes are not as good as theirs. It's better not to think about it. Let them call the shots. We won't determine what happens. Perhaps nothing will come of all this and it'll all blow over?"

In the mess hall there were also some reservists who had been recently called up. We began to practice field landings in earnest on our own airfield and on the small airfield of the aero club in Inowrocław. This intensive training was supposed to help us learn to utilize suitable field bases.

The squadron commander had received orders to prepare a whole network of field bases from which fighter units would be capable of undertaking operations in the case of conflict. Toruń was eventually surrounded by a ring of airfields extending out in all directions. And when Nazi Germany concluded a mutual assistance pact with Italy on May 22, 1939, peace seemed even less likely. The situation grew worse every day.

The eyes of the whole world were on Poland. Would it stand up to naked aggression?

Our country had a mutual assistance pact with England, concluded in August, as well as a secret military pact with France, concluded in the second half of May.

The secret military pact with France called for an immediate air offensive in the West in case of the outbreak of war. On the fifth day of war, an air offensive was to begin on the western border of Germany.

CHAPTER TWO

Pursuit of a Do-215

IT WAS FOUR O'CLOCK IN THE AFTERNOON. THE JUNE SUN BLAZED DOWN mercilessly making it stiflingly hot. I was lying on the grass in front of the station tent with Lieutenant Żulikowski, trying to escape the sun under the shade of some trees, waiting anxiously for the end of the day and our shift.

Suddenly Lieutenant Żulikowski noticed something and began to turn his head a little toward the sound locator.

"You got something there?" I couldn't help smiling.

"Shut up," he shouted, "Listen! I can hear an engine in the distance . . ."

I started to listen in intently.

"He's flying . . . very high altitude . . . in our direction, I think," he said.

We jumped out from under the trees to see if we could spot the plane in the sky. A distant murmur indicated its direction.

"There he is!" I yelled, pointing to the north in the direction of Bydgoszcz. "All you can see is his trail. He's very high . . . and coming in our direction . . . see."

"I'm going after him. There's no time to waste," I exclaimed in one breath, pulling on my helmet. "He's German!"

"Good, let's go!"

In an instant I was in my plane with the engine roaring. Advancing the throttle I turned the plane out of the bushes onto the airstrip, and in no time was airborne. In the air, I looked back over my shoulder and could see the German flying behind me. Keeping him in sight I tried to gain altitude, staying south of him. Every now and again I would glance at the altimeter as I pulled the plane up with all my might to gain as much altitude as I could across the enemy's path, which was ideally suited for my position.

My altimeter's needle moved ever so slowly: 5,000, 5,500 meters . . . The German continued to stay above and behind, but he didn't seem to see me. My altimeter already read 6,000 meters, but I didn't dare put on my oxygen mask because I was afraid of losing sight of him. I could clearly see, however, that he was a twin-engine plane. Below me was the dark ribbon of the Vistula River. The German was still about 200 meters above, as we rapidly drew closer together. My altitude was now 6,500 meters. The air became thinner, and it became increasingly difficult to breathe. My altimeter exceeded 7,000 meters, but the German continued on above me.

My plane became increasingly sluggish in its controls, and I began to sense a lack of oxygen. My breathing became rapid and short. I proceeded higher, using all my strength just to gain a little more altitude. I got closer to him. He was very fast. "I'll follow him by sight," I thought to myself, "he's almost directly above me." He was about 1,000 meters above, but I couldn't get any closer to him. After leveling off, I let up a little on the stick so as to gain speed. I was exhausted from the lack of oxygen. The German passed over me and sped away at a higher altitude. So I squeezed what was left out of the engine, climbing even higher to gain a few more meters. I recognized the silhouette on the twin rudders—it was a Do-215 with black crosses on the white backgrounds on its wings.

The Do-215, a long-range reconnaissance aircraft, cut right in front of me, and at that instant without thinking I fired. The traces of gunfire rent the air, chasing the unreachable enemy. I knew the distance and the difference in altitude were too great for my fire to have any effect. A torpor embraced my entire body, sweat began to form on my face, and my goggles began to fog up. I glanced at the altimeter: 7,900 meters! I looked again at the fleeing German plane and kicked my leg into the controls.

The plane, which lurched headfirst downward, quickly lost speed. I felt a sharp pain in my ears, which quickly became unbearable. "Maybe I better descend a little slower," I thought to myself. The needle on my

altimeter was dropping like crazy. After a while I slowly began to pull
the plane out of its dive. I felt a distinct relief, and my breathing returned
to normal—without palpitations. I didn't hear the sound of the engine
though—I was completely stunned. I swallowed a couple of times, at the
same time holding my nose to clear my ears. Finally I was able to hear
the muffled sound of my engine. . . .

Over the airfield I circled a couple of times to make a proper evaluation of altitude before landing.

When I had taxied into the hangar to refuel, I could see the wing
commander's car approaching. Colonel Stachoń rode right up to my
plane. I jumped out and reported my fruitless pursuit of the Dornier.

"Who opened fire, you or the Dornier?" he asked.

"I did," I said.

"Watching your pursuit from the ground we thought that you had
been shot down. We could see the traces of gunfire, and then heard their
sound, then we saw a plane tumbling straight down . . . what altitude were
you flying at?"

"7,900 meters, but the German was flying 600 to 700 meters higher."

"You were wearing your oxygen mask, of course?" he asked.

"Unfortunately, I didn't have time because I was afraid of losing sight
of him."

The colonel grabbed his head in disbelief.

"Are you crazy? Flying at that altitude without an oxygen mask!
Aren't you aware of the danger? Loss of consciousness can occur suddenly.
This is the second—and I hope last—time we will have this discussion!"

"Colonel, sir," I said, "every time it's different. Different circumstances, different situation, and so . . ."

He immediately interrupted me.

"I see that you are leaving yourself an opening for the future. Please
write a full report of your flight and give it to me tomorrow," he said.

I jumped on the truck, rode off, and returned to the command station.

The sun was approaching the horizon as dusk slowly fell. I was done for
the day.

"Wanna go to the Esplanade?" I asked Żulik as we returned from the airfield.

"That's what I was thinking," he replied. "You gotta have somewhere to relax and have a good time on Saturday."

We quickly figured out what we were going to do that evening, and parted company when we finally got to Żulikowski's apartment.

I walked leisurely away, step by step, smelling the potent fragrance of the flowers. From the Vistula I could feel the refreshing coolness of a spring breeze.

"Dammit I wish I could've reached him!" The German plane still bothered me.

We had already pursued so many German planes over Polish territory, and none of these pursuits had been successful. Today's was probably the best chance, and still no luck. They've really got to be laughing at us! We need faster planes with higher operational ceilings to be able to threaten them.

Warsaw was bombarded with such reports. Each contained the same depressing truth. But Warsaw remained silent, as if mesmerized. Why . . . ?

I finally arrived home, without finding answers to any of my questions.

A few days later Józef Żulikowski was reassigned to Dęblin as an instructor. Each time he read the order his face clearly showed his dejection. He looked vainly in every direction, as if looking for help, and then furiously threw the paper on the table. He cursed his misfortune in a way I had never heard from him before.

In the meantime, in preparing new exercises, the squadron commander composed a list of names specifying flight assignments.

We offered our condolences to Żulik who was still depressed. (I too stood under the threat of reassignment.) Captain Laskowski finally got up and left with Mirek to discuss the matter in private.

A short time later there was pandemonium in the pilots' annex. The news that another pilot was to be reassigned struck fear into all of us. We all wanted to stay with the unit. After our commanders settled us down, Mirek came in smiling.

"Don't worry," he told me, "as soon as we're in the air all your troubles will evaporate . . . let's get to work. There's not much time! We've been assigned to intercept and destroy a practice 'bombing raid' by some of our bombers." He showed me the target area on the map. "The squadron will be composed of three flights. Everyone will find their positions on the chart. We will attack in close formation, and remember not to break up the flights! Hand signals are known to everyone. We'll take off and land as a unit. Now let's get going, the bombers are already being rolled out."

The distinctive silhouettes of the P-23s were rolled out majestically, arranged in flights and squadrons for takeoff. Their engines resounded with a steady bass as the first squadron rose into the air. "They fly gracefully!" I sighed as I sat in my plane.

When they crossed the end of the runway again, I could hear the roar of their engines. The second group circled over the field to form up for the attack.

I still had to sit in my plane for a little while and wait my turn to take off. I looked at my watch.

"Clear!" I shouted to my mechanic.

"Clear!" he replied.

A blue smoke burst out of the exhaust pipes, the propeller blades hesitantly thwacking a few times. The engines coughed nervously, and then began to beat regularly in quick revolutions.

The squadron commander advanced out of the lineup of planes. I taxied after him as the number two plane. Nine planes in staggered formation rolled along to the end of the airfield. The three flights assembled themselves in line for takeoff. One after the other they raised their hands to signal they were ready . . . Mirek swung his head around and lowered his arm into the cockpit. The planes rolled forward and, gaining speed, took off in close formation.

At an altitude of 2,000 meters, and still climbing in formation, we flew off to meet the anticipated enemy. Half an hour later we reached the assigned region where we soon could see the dark silhouettes of the bombers below us. I couldn't help but notice how leisurely they flew in perfect formation.

Mirek began to maneuver, the squadron formed itself into a staggered formation to the right, and flight after flight dove to the attack with a great advantage of speed.

I followed right behind the squadron commander who attacked vigorously from close in. Upon finishing his attack, he looped downwards and to one side to shoot up in a chandelle, and after gaining altitude, repeated his attack. I kept with him, trying constantly to maintain the same distance. The fighters surged to the attack one after the other, after which they shot straight up like rockets to reform . . . a few attacks from the side and from the front did not break up the bombers. In fact, it even made them close their formations, which constituted their best defense. A solid enemy is hard to destroy, and our attacks did not produce results.

After completing the exercise the flights returned to their assigned positions and flew back to the base at treetop level. With the snub "noses" of the engines right above the treetops of the forest, we cut back on the throttles in order to land. The ground rumbled, and the gravel grated under the wheels of the planes landing in close formation.

Here and there an engine still growled and then . . . it was shut off. The pilots jumped out of their cockpits. The first thing, as usual, was to reach for a cigarette.

In the discussion of the attacks, Mirek criticized the flight commanders for attacks that were too spread out and weak, which is not how such attacks should be done.

"Only one plane stayed with me, and in every attack I had to wait for the rest," he continued. "Suddenness and continuity of attack in groups is the basis of success. Quick, powerful, and concentrated attacks deny the enemy and weaken his defensive formation's strength. Attacks must be furious. These individual attacks are useless."

After the debriefing we took a shower and, as our health regimen demanded, went out to the deck chairs for some rest.

That night we bid farewell to Żulik at the Esplanade's well-stocked bar. He was in a melancholy mood.

The second half of June began with a rash of fatal accidents in all our groups. It seemed as if a string of misfortunes had run through the entire air force. As a result, the Air Force Department suspended all flights for weeks, and the pilots were granted a two-week furlough.

I was among the first pilots to be furloughed. And whether I liked it or not—not being in the best financial position for such a venture—I had to leave for a rest. Of course, when you can't afford to go anywhere else you can always go home. And so that's what I did.

Summer was beautiful, perhaps a bit too hot and dry. And the sun burned my skin brown as I lay all day long in the sand on the banks of the Ikwa.

After the furlough was over, I reported back to the squadron commander. "Aren't you glad that I advised you to go on the first furlough tour," he said.

He laughed as he mentioned those who had planned to spend their furlough at seaside locations: in Jastarnia and Jurata.

"Look how sad you are!"

"Why?" I asked, not knowing why Mirek was laughing.

"What a flap! Furloughs have been suspended and the new orders prohibit absence from the base. So you see, it's best to take advantage of furloughs when you can get them. As things look now, we won't be getting any more furloughs until next year . . .

"Oh, well," he interrupted himself snickering, "we should get in some flying as long as it's still not too hot. You'll practice against Wieprzkowicz because he's been bugging me all day to go up against you. Three encounters, and then each can perform a selection of acrobatics. I'll discuss the assignment with you myself."

When we got together to put on our flying suits, I asked Corporal Wieprzkowicz, "What have you got against me?"

Wieprzkowicz leaned toward me, smiled broadly, and rubbed his hands with glee.

"I just want to see what you can do against me," he said, "and so far, I haven't had an occasion to. I just hope to be able to win one encounter."

"That's not much to ask. Why not win all three?" I said.

"If I can, I will," he replied. "But I see that we're just aggravating ourselves."

An hour later, after the exercise was over, and after we had taken a cold shower, all that the disconsolate Wieprzkowicz could do was grumble that his plane was poorer than mine.

"It constantly spun out," he declared. "Every time I pulled out of a spin I had to ease off on the throttle."

"You don't have to pull out so sharply that you lose speed entirely!" I said.

"Next time I'll choose a better plane so that I won't be embarrassed."

Wieprzkowicz had the strength of four. He could've worked two sticks at the same time, if this was only possible. But strength is not everything. Of course, it's necessary in a fight, but it's not the deciding factor. Every plane has its own individuality which the pilot has to take into account, which he has to learn in order best to adapt himself, and to create with it an inseparable, complementary whole. A mutual "understanding" is essential.

Often when you try to force a plane it doesn't respond. A misunderstanding arises, which is sometimes fatal for the pilot.

The shower made things better. The pilots returned from their exercises and immediately crowded under the streams of water, trying to relax after the confined and stifling cockpits of their planes.

A few days later we received a powerful infusion in the form of a detachment of about a dozen cadets from Dęblin as well as of non-coms from the secondary school in Krosno. Their education began immediately because we had to raise their proficiencies to the general level of the group.

A particularly valuable acquisition was Ensign Karol Pniak, who was attached to my squadron. An experienced hunter and excellent pilot, he was an alumnus of the group in Kraków. He belonged to the famous—in Poland—*Bajka trio* which included Captain Kosiński and Corporal Macki.

I was uneasy when the squadron commander assigned me to train him. I thought that he should really be teaching me. Karol staunchly protested however, modestly deprecating his knowledge of flying. He wasn't a conceited type by nature. And through his character, collegiality, and fame as a pilot, he quickly won our admiration and friendship. Before a flight we always wished him well. And after any exercise we didn't hesitate to commend him, which he fully deserved anyway. Karol would smile warmly, a little embarrassed, but always full of respect for his "superiors." He thought that rank was indispensable in the military. And he properly understood military discipline. In no time we became an inseparable part of the squadron commander's flight, which only brought us closer together. In this way we became close friends.

I also admired his wife, who was secretly married to him because junior officers were not allowed to be married. This was prohibited by strict military code. Neither he nor his wife, however, considered the implicit difficulties and exceptionally serious circumstances of married life. For many years Karol hid his marital status, and waited to the day of the outbreak of war before telling the group commander.

Ensign Jaugsch as well as Privates Spindel and Kosmowski showed promise for the future too. Their combat exercises were characterized by tenacity, intensity, and ambition, with great flying qualities.

At the end of July I flew with Władek Urban to the airfield in Gdynia, for the purpose of escorting a French plane that was flying to Poland via Copenhagen with the military mission of the French air force.

After two days wait we took off from Gdynia, flying over the sea, in the direction from which the French plane was to come. Our planes were completely armed. And in case of attack by Germans, it was left to our discretion whether to engage them. We were to escort the French plane through a dangerous sector to Grudziądz [Graudenz] where it was to land.

For some time we circled over the sea along the coast. The horizon was cloudy and visibility poor. The sea was completely bathed in a bluish mist. We flew around as if in a fish bowl.

Finally we could make out the dark silhouette of a large, twin-engine French plane in the fog. We closed in a tight V alongside the newcomer.

When we caught up to him, Władek tipped his wings in a sign of greeting. The clumsy, old Amiot bomber answered in kind.

Together we headed landward, with Władek taking the lead while Wejwer and I flew alongside the bomber. His pace was dreadfully slow. The old bucket dragged on at a snail's pace. We hung about him as if in agony. Finally, we reached our destination without encountering any Germans.

According to our orders the French plane was to land in Grudziądz. Instead, he continued on in the direction of Warsaw, completely ignoring our signals for him to land.

The Amiot circled the airfield at Grudziądz and then resumed his course for Warsaw. We gave up hope of getting him to land, and, considering that our assignment was completed, we took off for Toruń. It was only when we arrived at the base that we learned the French plane had decided to fly directly to Warsaw without refueling in Grudziądz.

Rumor had it that the French mission was to discuss problems connected with the preparation, on Polish territory, of a network of airfields for French heavy bombers. In case of war they were to take off from France, bomb German targets along the Polish border, and land here. This was the back-and-forth plan of bombing, employed by the British and Americans in the later phase of the European war. At the same time the Polish air mission was staying in Paris and London trying to purchase modern equipment in the form of British Hurricanes and Fairey Battle light bombers as well as French Morane-406 fighters.

Meanwhile, events moved apace. Toruń acquired a new, unfamiliar appearance. Windows were protected against bombing by taping white strips of paper to them. Parks, squares, and gardens were zigzagged with antiaircraft ditches. During nighttime alarms all lights were extinguished. The town was plunged into utter darkness, the streets were half empty, restaurants and bars were dead. It seemed as if most of the population had left town. At night it became increasingly apparent that military transports and trucks were passing through town in a northerly direction, toward the German border.

CHAPTER THREE

At the Field Base

ON THE 26TH OF AUGUST I HEARD A SUDDEN KNOCK ON MY DOOR. I jumped out of my bunk, ready to expel what I thought was an intruder— maybe a drunk who got lost on his way home. To my surprise in the half-open door I could see the face of the liaison officer.

"Lieutenant sir," he said, "general alarm! Please hurry, a car is waiting."

"I'll be ready in a minute," I replied, "after I've gotten myself together."

The group's bus was already teeming with people. I was the last one on, and then we drove off to the airfield. On the way we discussed the situation. There were all kinds of opinions. "Has it started already or not?"

We rushed to our operational areas. In no time work was begun on the preparation of the units for war. The seals were broken on top-secret envelopes, and hitherto secret orders were issued. Planes with full tanks of gas, fully armed, radio-equipped, ready for action rolled out from the fully lit hangars into the dark abyss of the night.

Before dawn, the 141st and 142nd Squadrons were ready to move into the field. Only the car carrying the pilots' personal baggage was still half-empty. It was finally filled in the afternoon.

At dawn we rolled all the planes in the group to the opposite end of the airfield, camouflaging them among the thickly scattered bushes adjoining the firing range where the radio car, which now acted as the command post, was stationed. The group was put in a state of combat-readiness, and the pilots of the designated signal flights stood ready by their planes.

During the morning hours all instructional and training aircraft were evacuated. Only bombers remained at the Toruń airfield.

The recently mobilized reserve pilots were taken by car to the region of Lida, Baranowicze, Wilno [Vilnius], and Słomin, where, in case of the outbreak of war, training centers were set up. The reconnaissance bombers were lined up at the north end of the field to protect them at the edge of the forest.

After the evacuation an uneasy calm ensued. The airfield appeared to be completely deserted. No planes could be seen anywhere. Only personal cars could be seen crisscrossing the field.

Inactivity prevailed, which was followed by an attendant boredom that is usually unbearable under such circumstances. Lying under our planes we contemplated many possibilities. As often happens in loneliness, we reflected on possible combat.

I looked to the future with confidence, however, and was ready to face any adversity. Whatever was to come fascinated, even excited me. Deep down inside I couldn't wait for it.

Despite everything, I underestimated German power and couldn't imagine that the events to come would take such a tragic turn. The magnificent fighting spirit of the group filled everyone with confidence.

Early on the morning of the 30th of August, the advance party of the ground crew set off for Markowo near Gniewkowo as its first stop.

During the morning hours the airfield was made ready. The roar of engines broke the silence, the clean silhouettes of the fighters emerged from the bushes, and the reconnaissance bombers were rolled out from the forest. The planes left their home bases and moved to field bases, never to return. The fighter group, arranged in flights, took off first. Trio after trio disappeared beyond the buildings of the city, in a westwardly direction.

I flew over the beautiful park in Bydgoszcz's suburbs, took off for the wild blue yonder, and crossed the Vistula near the bridge, looking for the last time on Toruń.

After a twenty-minute flight I landed at the field base, which was covered with a soft carpet of clover. The planes were camouflaged between trees lying alongside an old and unused road. In a short time antiaircraft positions were dug in. Their crews were armed with old Hotchkiss guns. Thereafter the group remained in a state of alarm. We pilots took up quarters in the town's old schoolhouse, while the ground crews commandeered nearby cottages and barns.

From that time on our source of sustenance was the field kitchen. The radio car, where the commander's post, as well as the operational and radio officer's, was to be found, was placed between the planes of both squadrons in a clearly visible spot for the signal-flight crews. A green rocket was established as the early warning signal. Details of orders were to be transmitted in name by radio after the planes were in the air. These contents were partially in code. The planes received their own code name—"bees."

The 30th and 31st of August passed peacefully. From the town in the distance, over the fields, an undisturbed silence prevailed, broken only by the sound of people shooting at empty bottles. This was the only concern for the signal flight. And so the last day of August came to a close. The sun disappeared over the horizon. Dusk fell quickly, and sentries were posted at intervals around the base.

We retired to quarters to spend our last night of peace.

At the same time advance airfields in East Prussia, Pomerania, Silesia, and Czechoslovakia were busy with their final preparations for attack.

"Case White"—the German invasion plan of Poland—was on the verge of realization. The decision had been made. Crews received their orders, flight routes were determined, meteorologists provided information about the weather, and maps and photographs of targets were studied.

Heinkels, Dorniers, and Junkers were loaded with bombs. Reconnaissance Henschels and Storches, and dangerously sleek Messerschmitts waited only for daybreak.

Even before dawn the air was rent by the sinister roar of thousands of planes, flying from the north, west, and south over sleepy Polish villages and towns, cities, aircraft factories, railway yards, bridges, and roads, coming to kill soldiers in their trenches, children in their cradles, old people and women.

At this time German military power had no equal in the world. The German General Staff was well organized. It was guided by the main elements of the Schlieffen Plan: the attempt to surround both flanks of the enemy, to strike at his rear, to attack with ferocity and surprise, and to concentrate force at decisive points. At the core of the Nazi armed forces was the largest land force ever, excellently equipped with the most modern weapons. It possessed overwhelming firepower.

Its real force, however, lay in its uncontestable offensive advantage. And the efficiency and military expertise of its operational staffs guaranteed the success of every action. At the same time, the German air force, which was the most powerful in the world, enjoyed the advantage of experience gained in the Spanish Civil War.

In contrast to this, the Polish military doctrine was determined by the Polish-Russian War of 1920 and prized the conception of mobile actions supported by a core of infantry divisions in conjunction with swift cavalry cooperation. It was only shortly before the war that a certain change in the right direction occurred. But unfortunately there wasn't enough time to reconstitute the whole of the armed forces, adapt them to carry out combat under different conditions, and equip them with modern weapons. Besides this, our operational staffs were an Achilles heel.

The Germans were already prepared for military action while their enemies were in the process of beginning the laborious and foreseeable mobilization of their armed forces.

Under pressure from France and England, Poland refrained from general mobilization. This delay, right up until the days before the attack, meant that only half of the Polish forces were mobilized. Only 45 percent of Polish forces were fully prepared.

The Germans hurled seven armored divisions, four motorized divisions, four light divisions, forty-seven infantry divisions, and one cavalry brigade at Poland. This constituted 85 percent of their total forces. In addition, two air fleets awaited orders to attack—3,500 planes.

The attack came on the 1st of September at dawn.

CHAPTER FOUR

First Combat

I FELT A SHARP TUG ON MY ARM. UPON OPENING MY EYES I COULD REC-
ognize the silhouette of Paweł Zenker in the darkness. He stood over
my bunk.

"Get up," he thundered, "you're on signal patrol!"

"Are you crazy?" I said. "It's still night. I can't see my hand in front
of my face . . ."

"Hurry up," he replied, "I can't help it. I'd like to be sleeping too. In
a half-hour it'll be dawn, and we have to grab something to eat. Hurry!"

Out the window all I could see was a thick black mist. "Why do
they have to bother us in such weather?" I thought to myself. "It's black,
it's foggy, and so they yank a guy out of a peaceful sleep." I jumped into
my pants and joined the other five who were waiting. After some strong
black coffee, we left in the truck for the airfield. In the distance I could
hear the roar of engines warming up. After arriving at the airfield, I
quickly climbed into my plane. It was warm and cozy, which was ideal
in light of the weather conditions, especially after the way in which my
sleep was interrupted.

I must have fallen asleep again because I was awakened by Sergeant
Wruś saying, "Please climb out, Lieutenant, I've brought breakfast," as he
unfolded a napkin beside the plane.

The sun began to heat things up, the fog burned off, and the horizon
gradually cleared up. I stretched my aching bones and started to eat.

"Any news, chief?" I asked the sergeant.

"Nothing right now. In the radio truck they're trying to get the morning communiqué."

I chatted a little more with Sergeant Wruś, and after breakfast I went over to the commander's post, where everyone was gathered, to find out how things stood. I had hardly arrived when Captain Laskowski jumped out of the radio car, flushed and excited. We all stopped talking and looked at him inquisitively.

"Are all the pilots here?" he turned to the squadron commanders.

"Yes!"

"Your attention please gentlemen," he spoke slowly and deliberately, "since five o'clock this morning we have been at war with Germany. Please maintain calm. Now with regard to our responsibilities . . . I sincerely believe that we will discharge them."

We received this news in silence, which was finally broken when Captain Laskowski said, "I would ask the squadron commanders to come with me."

Lieutenant Przymeński, the radio officer, briefed us on the contents of the communiqué. Warsaw, practically all permanent airfields, as well as important train stations had already been bombed. Since dawn, fighting had broken out along our entire frontier. The Germans were advancing on all fronts.

It was hard to believe. Each one of us was absorbed in his own thoughts, but the meager information didn't supply enough material for discussion. One way or another we were all disturbed. This was clear from the way everyone was puffing on their cigarettes. Without a word we all left for our planes. The camouflaged Jedenastkas looked like greyhounds lying in wait for the signal to leap to the hunt. The ground crews lay next to them ready to respond to any order.

"In the meantime, Stasiu, we ought to practice on some bottles," Karol Pniak said. We had already drawn signal flight duty, with Corporal Wieprzkowicz.

"Okay, but where did you set up your 'shooting gallery?'" I asked.

"Over there, so that no one would use it. Here, put this bottle on that stump."

"Where? on yourself?"[1] I asked. Karol smiled at my allusion to his name.

"Oh please!" he said, "in that case put it on that broken tree over there."

"Well that changes things," I said.

In any case we put on our parachutes, which didn't interfere with our game as Karol went first. The bottles exploded and glass flew everywhere.

The fog finally lifted to reveal a broken sky. All around there was silence interrupted only by the abrupt bang of our pistol shots. The noise of the war hadn't reached us yet. For us it was something unreal, lying in wait for us somewhere far away. I was just lining a bottle up in the sights of my own pistol when the mechanic shouted, "To your planes!"

In a moment I turned around to see the green rocket shooting up against the background of the fluffy, snow-white clouds. I threw my pistol on the ground and jumped into the cockpit of my plane. I hooked up my straps, the engine roared, and my Jedenastka rolled out onto the open field of fresh, dew-drenched clover.

While gaining altitude, I headed in the direction that the radio reported the enemy was to be found. I flew northeasterly over patches of whirling clouds at an altitude of 1,500 meters, looking around for the enemy, for my first enemy encounter! Behind me followed the other two Jedenastkas. Since the sky was clear at the altitude I was flying, I decided to move the search below, descending through gaps in the clouds. Before reaching the Vistula, however, where the clouds had almost completely disappeared, I suddenly saw before me, at low altitude, the distinctive silhouette of an enemy plane. I switched on my radio and radioed to the others, "Attention, Henschel 126, direction—Port Drzewny, altitude—50-100 meters." At the same time I eased the plane into a dive to attack.

The German reconnaissance plane flew calmly in a straight line. Its crew was evidently preoccupied with ground reconnaissance, because it

---

[1] Skalski is humorously referring here to the fact that the word *pniak* means "stump" in English.

paid no attention to what was happening around them in the sky. The distance between us closed rapidly.

"He still doesn't see me," I thought to myself. His calmness disturbed me so much that I could feel a shiver run through my entire body. After a while I opened fire. A few more seconds . . . and I could see the black cross insignias on his plane distinctly. They grew; they blinded me. I held them in my gun sight, making gradual adjustments.

Suddenly the Henschel's observer opened fire at me chaotically. The pilot went into a quick dive in an attempt to flee. The traces of gunfire enveloped my entire plane like an octopus. I pushed the stick forcefully. And keeping him in my sights I drew even closer to him than before.

250 meters . . . 200 . . . 150 . . . still closer. I thought—now!

I squeezed the trigger. The Vickers guns fired flawlessly. "I'm right on his tail," I thought, "no need to adjust." A long burst stopped the observer's fire, and his propeller slowed down dramatically. A fraction of a second later—and a final short burst from right on top of him. Then I pulled up sharply to avoid crashing into him and the fire of Lieutenant Pisarek and Corporal Mielczyński, who were also on his tail. After making a half-turn I could see that the pilot of the Henschel was trying to find a suitable place to land the plane. It didn't look as though the plane was being skillfully piloted, and I guessed the pilot must have been wounded. The Henschel rolled and bounced like it was out of control until finally, after having tumbled on the soft, newly plowed field, it flipped over onto its back.

The Jedenastkas performed a *danse macabre*, circling for a while over their victim. Still affected by the fight, however, and without thinking, I circled round and came in for a landing, forgetting how dangerous it was to land on such difficult terrain. Fortunately things went well. After a while my plane, jolted by the uneven terrain, came to a stop near the Henschel that had crashed. There was quiet all around. All the other planes had flown off. The only sound was that of the engine of my plane idling. I quickly jumped out of my plane and ran to the crash site. Suddenly a thought stopped me, and I turned around and ran just as quickly back to my plane to shut off its engine. The idea of the German pilot escaping in my plane seemed fantastic, but I wanted to preclude such a possibility anyway. Preventing him from starting up my engine would prevent me from becoming the butt of unpleasant jokes, so I hid the starter handle under the seat and only then did I return to the Henschel.

I expected to find the crew inside the plane, wounded or dead. But the seats were empty, and both cockpits were full of blood. I immediately began to look for the Germans. Along the path of the forced landing, at a distance of about 15 meters on the opposite side of a small brook, I could see the white canvas of a parachute spread out—and a body lying on it. I leaped over the brook and found myself facing the war's first victim. The German was lying on his back, covered with blood and unconscious. His mouth was open, covered with foam, bloody, and grunting. Apparently when the plane crashed the pilot was thrown out, the parachute hooked onto something, and opened by itself.

However, the other member of the crew was nowhere to be found.

Some local people, attracted by the sight of the combat and the crash of the German plane, came running from different directions across the field to the accident scene. For a little while longer I looked about carefully, scouring the neighboring undergrowth, but there was no evidence of the person I was looking for. I then decided that, in the meantime, I would try to help the wounded German as much as I could. I had just rolled up the parachute and placed it under him so that it would be a kind of bed when the first curious onlookers arrived. I asked them to search the edge of the distant woods where the other German was probably hiding. All the men ran off in that direction. A woman remained and helped me carry the wounded German onto the makeshift bed. Then I turned my attention to the wrecked Henschel, in which I had previously seen a first-aid kit. I broke the glass case and collected its entire contents of bandages, cutting instruments, syringes, and medicines about whose use I didn't have the faintest idea. With the knife I cut away the sleeve of the uniform and shirt, carefully removing all the wounded man's clothes. He had been shot through the shoulder—a serious wound that was gushing blood. Helped by the local woman, I washed the pilot's face with the clear stream water, poured iodine on the wound, after which, applying some swabs, I bandaged the wound as tightly as possible to stop the bleeding.

We were in the process of moving the wounded pilot when, at the sound of something moving, I suddenly glanced at the neighboring shrubs. I put the pilot down, got up from my knees, and looked about intently. This time there was no doubt. I detected the distinct silhouette of a man in a flying suit the color of which was barely distinguishable from the surrounding greenery.

I jumped a couple of steps forward and shouted out the only German word I knew: "halt!" after which I added, in Polish, "*ręce do góry!*" ["hands up!"]. At the same time I reached into my pocket for my pistol but grabbed my cigarette case instead. It was only then that I remembered I had thrown my pistol on the ground when we had scrambled.

I had to make a decision, so I quickly drew the cigarette case out of my pocket, and pretending it was a gun advanced on the unsuspecting German. He didn't move, raised his arms with difficulty, and limping a little, willingly stepped out of the undergrowth. I then lowered my hand so that he wouldn't see that my "weapon" was only a cigarette case. Seeing that he couldn't escape I approached him. I took his pistol away, and offered him a cigarette from the cigarette case. He smiled through his pain, nodded to me, and taking the cigarette, stammered "*danke schön*." At that moment my fears evaporated: An injured German would be in no position to harm me or to flee. After having him place his hands behind his head, I escorted him back to the other German. I placed him beside his comrade on the unfurled parachute, gave him a pack of cigarettes and matches, and went back to attending to his countryman.

When I slowly raised the left arm of the wounded pilot—at the same time supporting the right on the ground so that the woman could stretch the bandage—the other German who observed the whole procedure leaned forward and quite unexpectedly kissed my hand. I recoiled as if scalded. For a brief moment our eyes met. I'd say that my eyes expressed nothing but surprise, but in his I saw an expression of gratitude. We exchanged smiles, and I knew that my responsibility as a human being required me to finish what I had started. Due to the tragedy of war, he became someone different—the one who brought us together.

"I'll finish this one myself," I said to the woman, "why don't you attend to the other in the meantime." She grabbed a knife and leaned over the second patient. But this one began to say something very rapidly in a language incomprehensible to us. From his gestures, however, we figured out that he was protesting.

"What's the matter?" I asked in Polish, looking in his direction.

"I don't know," replied the startled woman. "He doesn't seem to want me to touch him."

"No, no, the pilot!" cried out the German pointing to me.

I smiled understandingly. The woman shrugged her shoulders and helped me in placing and covering the first German.

In the meantime the people who earlier had gone out to look for the missing German returned and gathered around us. They started to become a mob and began to murmur threateningly at the Germans. "Better to string them up by their ankles with their heads in the water than to help them out." "To hell with 'em." "Because of them I have to leave home tomorrow. I've been drafted."

They became ugly. Among the spectators I spied someone wearing a railway man's uniform. "Do you work for the railroad?" I asked.

"Uh-huh," he muttered hesitantly.

"Run to your station and telephone the district hospital in Toruń. Please tell them that, at my request, they send an ambulance for the wounded airmen. Tell them what's happened here. One of the wounded Germans is not hurt badly. No bones are broken, and he's not bleeding profusely. I'll soon be finished with bandaging his wounds."

Nearby I could see a figure in dark clothing approaching, and I could tell he was a clergyman. He looked in silence at the wounded airmen for a little while and then turned to me.

"Lieutenant sir, would you allow me to offer these men some spiritual comfort, especially the seriously wounded one. I am a German and the pastor in this area."

I agreed, and the pastor addressed the healthier and conscious airman in German. He talked for a long time, but I couldn't understand what he was saying. The pilot, however, brushed the priest off, said something brief and sharp to him, and walked away. The pastor looked at me angrily. Then he turned his attention to the more seriously wounded airman, and with an expression of sympathy spread his arms out in a gesture of helplessness. He apologized to me and asked to leave. It was then that I asked him what the wounded airman had said to him.

"He didn't want any solace or kind words from me. He told me that I should turn my attention to the other."

I looked in the eyes of the old man, and he looked down at the ground, obviously ashamed. We didn't say anything. He took my hand and shook it a couple of times.

"It's difficult to look at what has happened," he whispered in distress. "As a pastor and a German I would like to thank you, lieutenant, for what you have done. May God take care of you."

He bowed and slipped away slowly and deliberately.

I started to go through the pockets of my captives. Properly speaking, I should have done this first, but I thought that my first obligation was to help the wounded.

I discreetly removed the "wings" and insignia from the pilot's collar, which I allowed myself as an innocent larceny. In the pockets of one of my captives, I found some letters and photographs of two ordinary-looking, blonde-haired girls, and the pilot's and observer's identity cards. Both of these men were the same age as I. One came from Darmstadt, the other from Königsberg. The one who was conscious carefully watched my every action. When I gathered up all of the, from the military point of view, worthless loot he turned to me and said something I couldn't understand, pointing at the things I had in my hands. The only word I understood was "*Fräulein*." And the imploring look on his face helped me to understand his request. I gave him back his identity card, letters, and photographs. I told him in Polish, "I'll keep the insignia and wings as a souvenir." The delighted German jabbered something of which I could only understand "*danke schön*." We then exchanged cigarettes, and I could tell he was satisfied.

I jumped back across the brook and made my way through the people who had gathered at the plane that had crashed. I had to convince one of the farmers whose horse had been shot that this must have been done by one of our planes because the Germans had only shot in an upwards direction at us. I also tried to convince the crowd that hanging the unarmed Germans was not the right thing to do. I told them that these Germans were no threat to them, and that they should save their energy for those who would follow—the ones who were powerful and well armed. The farmers began to discuss this among themselves.

"You're right, lieutenant, we agree. We've seen scoundrels like these coming towards Toruń since dawn, and the people are angry. But if we haven't harmed them by now we probably won't," they assured me.

A little time had to pass before I saw the ambulance coming toward us across the fields. The accompanying sergeant put the wounded in the ambulance and, after reporting to me, took off with them.

I then began to search the wreck of the Henschel. I found forage-caps, gas masks, two cameras, and more importantly—two maps in different scales designating regions of reconnaissance. Various details concerning probable directions of German attacks were marked on them. Thus the reconnaissance plane proved to be a valuable find. I carefully washed the maps of blood, and afterwards dried them off. I then took them to my own plane. I decided to fly directly to the airfield in Toruń to deliver the maps as soon as possible to the army headquarters there. My only worry was whether I would be able to land, because I knew that the airfield had already been severely bombed.

Since the crowd of spectators didn't leave after the wounded Germans had been taken away—apparently waiting for more to happen—I asked them to help me get my plane ready for takeoff. They willingly agreed, and we went off together in the direction of my plane. When I saw the condition of the field, however, I got so angry that I cursed myself for being so stupid as to land on such a bunch of potholes. The field was too short for a takeoff, and worse, there were trees in every direction. The ground was soft because it had been recently plowed. But there wasn't anything better in sight, which meant that there was no chance of moving the plane to another, more suitable, place. So I decided to try to take off where I was.

I scrambled into the cockpit, turned on the engine, and advanced the throttle to turn the plane completely around. It didn't budge. I advanced the throttle further and the tail began to vibrate. I advanced the throttle even more, but the plane still didn't move. It stood there as if it were planted. I was furious. So I turned off the engine, undid my straps, and jumped out. The wheels were completely submerged in the soft ground. It would be impossible to extricate them. With the people's help, however, I was able to dig them out, after which I showed them how to raise the tail and swing the plane around in the opposite direction. I then jumped back into the cockpit, and the plane was finally placed in the right direction for takeoff. I instructed that one wheel should be put in the rut along the ridge dug by the plough. This made it possible to support part of the undercarriage on whatever hard surface there was. Once again I looked with trepidation at the field and its copse of birch trees.

I slowly released the brake and advanced the throttle. When the tail began to budge and rise up, I released the brake completely, moving the throttle ahead ever so slowly at the same time. The freed plane, rocking along the uneven, muddy terrain with a slight bank to the right, began to roll and slowly gathered speed. The trees began to draw near alarmingly. I didn't sense enough speed to lift the plane off the ground, though. So I pulled back a little on the stick, making a quick estimate of the distance, and with no other choice, against better judgment, decided to try to take off. The plane shook and the wheels skipped several times along the ridges. I was off. With all my might I pulled up at the minimal speed, fearing that I'd hit the trees. The treetops flashed by, and I could hear their branches scraping against the undercarriage and fuselage. Tenderly they reached out to the plane, as if trying to drag it down.

Fifteen minutes later I was circling over the systematically bombed airfield in Toruń looking for some part of it on which I could land. Finally I set down on the moor adjoining the airfield, ending up on a road. My colleagues were very proud when I tossed them the German cap and the other trophies of the fight.

The air-defense flight was stationed at the airfield under the command of Lieutenant Jan Czapiewski. When I climbed out of my plane, he was standing there with his head bandaged. He explained that during the bombardment he was hit in the ear by a flying fragment.

"Can you imagine, it hit me almost in the middle of the airfield while I was running to my plane," he said. "It was really something! I didn't know what to do. I hugged the ground, and their bombs fell all around me like peas. A real hell!"

As I left I could still hear him cursing the man with the little moustache.

During the bombardment several people had been killed and wounded. The barracks, where there were a lot of people, were very hard-hit.

Our conversation was interrupted when the jeep arrived to take me to the Pomorze army headquarters. When I got there I made a brief report to Colonel Stachoń, who was the commander of air forces in the area, and handed over the maps as well as the photographic equipment. The information contained in the maps seemed to be extremely valuable and was immediately sent to the operations center. After having to listen to some sarcastic remarks from the colonel concerning my recent Samaritan efforts, dinner, and receiving some orders for Captain Laskowski, I returned to the airfield to take the air-defense flight to its next base. Unfortunately, however, because of darkness and fog we were not able to land there and had to return to Toruń. I spent that night in the camp adjoining the southern extreme of the airfield. As soon as I got into my firm, comfortable bed I was able to relax and go over the day's events in my head. Then I was able to think about what was to come, because in the heat of combat I had completely forgotten that we were at war. The concentration and intensity required of combat had so consumed my attention that I had lost the ability to think about anything else. Everything however—the "how, if, and when" that I thought about that night—had to remain, for the time being, unanswered. I experienced the unbearable weight of uncertainty.

Next morning I returned to my base without incident. Captain Laskowski had already learned about my actions from Colonel Stachoń, and he categorically forbade me to repeat any such actions in the future.

"By the way," he added, "your captives could not find words enough to thank you for the care you gave them. They asked for your name. In fact, they were so insistent that I had to give them an answer, which, I believe, will do you no harm if you ever experience a fate similar to theirs."

I was gratified by this. Besides, Laskowski's scenario was not altogether unlikely. The war had just begun.

CHAPTER FIVE

Victory and Loss

CAPTAIN LASKOWSKI ANNOUNCED A BRIEFING TO TAKE PLACE AT TWO o'clock for the pilots of both squadrons. After he left we spread out our leather coats on the grass and, lying down on them, began to speculate on the subject of the forthcoming briefing. From time to time we could hear the mechanics testing an engine. I listened intently to their performance. An engine would rev up and then suddenly subside, while armorers worked on the planes' guns and synchronization mechanisms.

Our chatting was interrupted by the call to dinner where Captain Laskowski wasted no time in satisfying our curiosity. Both squadrons had received new orders. The first was a squadron sweep of the Grudziądz-Łasin region at an altitude of 2,000 meters. The second was a low-level attack on a group of German armored units—whose presumed position would be given later—advancing in the direction of the Vistula. And this attack was to be carried out by an entire squadron. Laskowski emphasized that the assignment was difficult, but that the army commander—although aware of our limited capabilities as well as of the enemy's formidable antiaircraft defense—requested its execution at all cost. This attack had as its purpose to maintain the morale of our army.

"Who wants to volunteer to attack the armor column?" he asked.

The room filled with silence. So I whispered to Mirek: "Let's do it!"

He looked at me and shook his head no, after which he whispered to me, "That's insane! I'll go, but only if they assign it to me."

Captain Laskowski finally broke the silence.

"Okay then, I'll lead the 141st Squadron on the ground attack, and the 142nd Squadron under Captain Leśniewski will do the sweep. Take-off at three o'clock. The 141st first and the 142nd second. Briefing of the pilots of the 141st Squadron in fifteen minutes. Captain Leśniewski will brief the 142nd on his own."

I couldn't understand why a squadron of light bombers was not assigned to bomb the tanks. They were actually in a better position to inflict more damage on the armored columns, and without exposing themselves to the threat of heavy losses. Unfortunately, a different decision had been made, and the 141st Squadron had to bear the burden of it on their backs. Mirek was right to speak of insanity.

A few minutes before 3:00 we were sitting in our planes waiting for the 141st Squadron to take off. The first flight to take off included Captain Laskowski, Lieutenant Urban, and Corporal Jeka. When they had taken off they were immediately followed by the flight including Captain Rolski, Lieutenant Różycki, and Corporal Budziński. The third flight was commanded by Lieutenant Pisarek with Lieutenant Jankowski and Corporal Mielczyński. The entire squadron made a low pass over our heads in a V, and then took off in the direction of the target. We watched them for as long as we could.

The 142nd Squadron took off in the following order: first flight— Captain Leśniewski, me, and Ensign Pniak; the second flight—Lieutenants Wilczewski and Zenker, and Ensign Kogut; the third flight—Lieutenant Zieliński, and Corporals Wieprzkowicz and Łysek.

Gaining altitude we flew off in a northeasterly direction.

We crossed the Vistula north of Toruń at an altitude of 1,500 meters. Mirek headed off in the direction of the sweep. We flew at different altitudes as the clear blue sky sparkled in the sunlight and the air was calm. Far off in the distance on the right I could see Chełmża. I paid careful attention to my left because I thought this would be the most probable direction from which enemy planes might appear. Against the background of the Vistula, beside the bridge at Fordoń, I could see the advancing silhouettes of large planes, lying to the south. They were advancing at about a 90-degree angle to us, and slightly behind. I instantly looked toward Mirek and, dipping my wing to get his attention,

I signaled him the direction. At the same time I made a deep, slow turn toward the Germans. In this way I hoped to be able to indicate the enemy's location and make the other planes follow me. But I didn't look back to see if they had followed me because I didn't want to lose sight of the enemy planes. Besides, I was convinced that Mirek would follow with the rest of the squadron to the attack. The Germans were still a little ways off when I realized that they were farther below me than I had thought. So I cut the gas and slipped down, carefully following the enemy advance.

"I hope they don't turn, that's the only chance I have of getting close enough to them for a frontal attack! If they turn I won't be able to catch up with them . . . ," I thought to myself. The Germans advanced in two tight Vs, with seven planes close behind. The distance between us decreased, and I could tell that they were Dornier-17s. A few more side-slips and I was at their altitude, closing directly on them for the attack. I slowed down a bit to give myself the chance of having a longer period of fire. The Dorniers got bigger and bigger, becoming gigantic. It seemed as if they wanted to be attacked without changing course. I then concentrated all my attention on my gun sights, taking aim at the leading plane, which continued on undisturbed. The rings of my gun sight skipped along the pilot's cockpit.

Suddenly the Germans opened a seemingly impenetrable barrage of fire. Traces of gunfire surrounded me like a cobweb. Instinctively I closed my eyes and crouched in my cockpit trying to reduce the target I made. I was seized by a strange paralysis. For a moment I felt an anxiety that paralyzed my entire nervous system. I clenched my teeth in a painful contraction.

After a little while I shook it off, came to my senses, and, ignoring everything going on around me, concentrated my attention on the plane filling my gun sights. Three hundred meters . . . 200 meters—the Dornier grew to immense proportions. I heard the rattle of his machine guns before I even realized he had opened fire. I held off firing a long burst to the last moment, and then I broke off into a dive. The huge, white bellies of the bombers flashed before my eyes. Pulling up from my dive, I saw a Dornier coming down. So I turned and pursued him at full speed, not really understanding what was happening. The plane was diving at too steep an angle, which indicated that it was out of control. I closed in from behind in the event that the German should pull out, but unfortunately he didn't. I broke off the pursuit and pulled back as strongly as I could on the stick. Nothing now could prevent the German from crashing. I leveled off above the Dornier as it crashed into the ground at full speed. The explosion and enormous column of fire in the form of an inverted cone proclaimed the end of the drama. The powerful blast that shook my plane confirmed that the Dornier was carrying a full load of bombs.

I now carefully scoured the sky. The flight of bombers that had been broken up by my attack now tried to reform as I returned. Since I was below them, I tried to gain altitude as quickly as possible. They in turn tried to form up by circling. But I attacked the last plane, which was trying to circle-up, from behind, and from the most advantageous position, from out of the sun. With a few short bursts, I opened fire from about 150 meters, closing the distance to 50 meters while turning. Its gunner stopped firing even before I had already come out of the sun's trajectory. The Dornier's right engine caught fire and smoke was pouring out of the fuselage, trailing a long, mournful ribbon behind the plane. Finally two short bursts from close in and the Dornier tumbled down, falling out of the circle of planes in which it had sought refuge. I immediately jumped aside and watched the burning plane. And in a moment it was all over.

The Dornier crashed into the ground. None of its crew survived.

Climbing again I noticed that I was alone. I couldn't find any of the remaining Germans anywhere. But before long I looked west and saw the silhouette of a lone Dornier, which was trailing a thin ribbon of smoke, trying to gain altitude on its way home. Obviously hit, and not being able to keep pace with the rest of his group, he had decided to find his own way back to the "*Vaterland.*" He crept upward persistently. From 3,000 meters all I could see were the remaining four Dorniers far above the bridge at Fordoń.

Columns of water caused by explosions indicated that the bombers had hurriedly dropped their bombs, as was to be proved later, without causing the least damage.

I could also see another Jedenastka behind and below me. I suspect that it must have been the one that had attacked the fleeing Dornier. I didn't see the third plane. This didn't stop my pursuit of the fleeing enemy, however. At first, the distance between us decreased. But after a while I noticed with frustration that I constantly remained about 800 meters behind, and not able to overtake him. I therefore had to make a decision.

My altimeter already read 6,000 meters. On my right I could see Bydgoszcz. The sun was shining directly in my eyes making it difficult to see. The Dornier's silhouette against the background of the murky, gray slurry became ever smaller, constantly pushing on above. It would probably be pointless to continue the pursuit. Besides, I didn't have oxygen, and the altimeter already read 6,500 meters. I therefore gave up any further, senseless pursuit.

I dipped my wing to my "shadow" behind me, and took off. This adventure without oxygen was a real ordeal.

At an altitude of about 3,000 meters I began to circle to allow my unknown companion to catch up.

After a while I could recognize Wacka Wilczewski scrunched up in his cockpit. I waved to him, and descending together we made for home. Time now was critical—we were almost out of gas.

Circling the airfield I could see a lot of commotion on the ground among the pilots and mechanics of our squadron. It was as active as a beehive. We were the last of the group to land. When I climbed out of my plane all the pilots ran over. Mirek with his face all excited called out to me from a distance:

"Hey! How'd you do?"

When I told him that I had shot down two Dornier-17s, he clapped me on the back. He was as happy as a kid.

"Do you know how many we shot down altogether, and without any losses? Seven Dorniers, my boy, not counting the damaged ones. That's splendid work. And you wanted to attack the tanks."

I was surprised by the good news.

"Where, when?" I asked, "Because I didn't see anyone but Wacka, so . . ."

Mirek just continued to smile.

"Yeah, yeah, I know," he said, "I saw you waving your wings, but I didn't pay any attention to it. I was preoccupied with the nine Dorniers straight ahead of us. Then another, completely different group turned up."

"Yeah. We had to deal with two different groups at the same time. Of the nine we attacked only four were able to escape, we shot down five."

"Who?" I asked.

"Pniak, Kogut, and Wieprzkowicz each got one, and I got two. That's it, my friend."

Then his expression changed.

"This Dornier-17 is a nasty article. It was a chilling experience when it turned: a long and bright belly just like an over-turned crocodile. It made my skin crawl . . . brr . . ."

"Lieutenant, sir," the mechanic turned to me, "perhaps you would want me to examine your plane? It should be inspected. It has some minor holes, but it's not too bad. You had a close shave. In fact, you might very well be sitting somewhere in a field right now, if not worse. . . ."

Only then did I remember that right after the first encounter my engine sounded a little strange, different. For a moment then I thought that I would have to turn back, but since my gauges all seemed normal my fears quickly evaporated, and I forgot all about it. This only goes to show that the ear is not the worst instrument, and sometimes more sensitive than precision devices. Holes in the wings, a punctured undercarriage strut, and a damaged cylinder that caused the change in the engine's sound—no real serious damage. The plane didn't need special attention.

The planes of the 141st Squadron, however, did not present an equally agreeable picture. They encountered a veritable wall of fire, and not only from machine guns, but also from cannons. Only in the debriefing did we learn about the outcome of the encounter. Three of our pilots were killed, one crashed. Mirek was right not to be anxious to attack the armored columns. The result of both encounters—in the air and on the ground—was only too telling. It was clear that German antiaircraft fire was very potent and effective against light, non-armored planes. A direct hit in a cockpit not protected from behind by armor or by bulletproof glass in the windscreen meant the pilot's death or at least a serious wound.

While we were discussing the results of both encounters Lieutenant Skiba, our squadron's tactical officer, appeared. He interrupted our discussion to remind us how necessary it was to complete the debriefing as quickly as possible because the results had to be sent to headquarters the same day. We had to complete this drudgery before we could return to our comrades in the 141st Squadron.

After the debriefing we immediately fell into a swirl of heated discussion. Corporal Jeka, who flew in the first flight with Laskowski and Urban, gesticulating frantically, re-created the situation at the moment of attack.

"We came upon the Germans so suddenly that I believe we were both caught by surprise. Tanks, various types of vehicles, and people mixed together in one confused mass. They were grouped together in large units bivouacked in the open field, no camouflage whatsoever. They didn't seem to be concerned about an air attack at all. I was in the trailer position, with Captain Laskowski and Lieutenant Urban ahead of me. They opened fire, almost at the same time, on the tanks and their crews who ran like a swarm of locusts, falling all over themselves and seeking shelter behind their vehicles. Even though they were completely surprised, the Germans immediately opened a hellish fire from their different types of antiaircraft weapons. It was really hot. We were surrounded on all sides by white traces; and explosions of artillery fire closed off any exit from the hell. I followed Captain Laskowski and Lieutenant Urban, hacking my way through until I exhausted my ammunition, and then I swung completely around. I tried to fly as low as possible, almost scraping the ground, trying to avoid being hit. Everything happened so fast that it almost seemed unreal. Captain Laskowski was hit almost immediately, in the first stage of the attack. His plane suddenly caught fire and crashed into the Germans. After hitting the ground at full speed, the engine split off and pieces of the burning plane flew into the air. I think that the captain must have been hit right away because I saw his plane go down out of control. It was a frightening experience. I had barely turned to fly past the smoking remnants of his plane when I could see Lieutenant Urban's plane slowly coming up from its attack . . . and then flipping over on its left. It wasn't on fire, but it crashed full speed into a tank and burst into flames. Nothing remained of it."

Corporal Jeka then paused, lighting a cigarette with trembling hands.

"So . . . ," he added, "Captain Laskowski and Lieutenant Urban won't be coming back."

Silence hung over the gathering.

After a moment Jeka continued:

"I don't know by what miracle I came out of that cauldron in one piece. I flew off in one direction for some time before deciding to turn back home. I didn't see any of our planes anywhere. It was only above the Vistula that I came upon a strange-looking plane. I pushed my throttle forward and catching up with it I could see the silhouette of a damaged-Jedenastka. Getting closer, I could recognize Jankowski. The seriously damaged plane had a perforated fuselage, and a large part of the tip of the left wing had been completely shot off, which was the reason for its strange silhouette. Jankowski's vacant expression told me that he was still shaken by what he had just gone through, just as I was. We flew together for some time. Since Jankowski was heading in the direction of Sierpc I kept close to him and tried to indicate the correct way home. He didn't react to my signals, however, and continued to fly in the same direction. In view of this I left him and returned by myself. I don't know what made him fly in the opposite direction."

"And what happened to Mielczyński, what flight was he in?" asked Mirek.

"Mine," replied Marian, "I don't know what happened to him. After the attack I didn't see either of my wingmen—Mielczyński or Edka. From what Jeka has said, however, it seems that Jankowski is still alive. As for Mielczyński, I think he was shot down. But I'm not sure . . . maybe he'll still return? Maybe he was just damaged and forced to land somewhere . . . to hell with these methods of 'maintaining morale!'" he suddenly declared.

We all agreed with his harsh remark.

"I don't understand," added Marian, "what's going on in the minds of our commanders? To deprive our light bombers of such a suitable assignment. To squander an occasion that will never return. Now the Germans will be more alert. Instead, as if out of spite, against all logic, they send us with a couple "fire-engines" against a pile of iron. Any more brilliant ideas like this and we'll all be dead!"

We couldn't find any justification for the exceptionally irrational use of poorly armed and unarmored fighter planes for this type of action. The brass had decided it without any experience in and knowledge of the principles of air operations. But in war such mistakes are paid for with blood. No force is able to overcome or withstand the consequences of mistakes. The price that the soldier pays for the incompetence of his commanders seemed to be too high to us.

We continued to pass the time in such discussions until the sun went down, sitting under the trees dissecting the events of the day. We also considered whom to appoint to the unfortunately open positions of group and squadron commander.

Suddenly Paweł jumped up and cried "Junkers-87, look!" pointing in the direction of Toruń.

In the indicated direction, far on the horizon, against the background of the graying sky, I could see a plane's dark silhouette approaching. The Junkers-87 almost seemed to be an illusion. It was flying low in a southerly direction, as if following the Vistula. Marian and Leszek Lachowicki quickly jumped into their planes waiting for the command to intercept. But there was a moment's hesitation because opinions were divided regarding the silhouette of the poorly visible plane. Finally, Captain Rolski gave the signal to take off. In no time Marian and Leszek were flying low at full throttle trying to intercept the plane which, in the meantime, had circled round slowly to the west. We watched the pursuit intently. We could see its complete development in the wide-open sky. The distance between the pursued plane and our fighters rapidly decreased. It seemed to us that the German did not see the attacking planes. He didn't react to the rapidly approaching danger at all.

Someone cried out, "You're on his tail, open fire!"

Marian came further down, and then pulled up to attack. We could see his guns firing in the traces of smoke. He then shot up in a chandelle and turned around. We lost sight of the enemy. Both Jedenastkas circled for a while and then returned to base.

"That was perfect," said Karol with admiration, after the tension had passed. "Beautiful attack! One burst and it was all over."

We ran over to the plane that had just landed and taxied around to its place under the trees. Captain Rolski was the first to congratulate Marian on his quick victory.

"You really do us credit!"

But Marian just looked at us strangely from his plane. He didn't say anything at first. He lit a cigarette, took a deep drag and suddenly cursed vilely.

"Do you know who I shot down?!" he yelled.

"A Junkers-87," everyone answered.

"No, not a Junkers, dammit," he burst out laughing hysterically, "but one of our own bombers! I was so mesmerized by this damned Stuka that, staring at its markings and its silhouette from close in, I didn't recognize it. But after the attack, when I watched the plane make a forced landing, my hair stood on end. Thank God everyone survived. But it seems that someone in the plane must have been hit because he needed help to get out ..."

"Did you fire too?" he turned to Leszek, "I didn't notice."

"Fortunately, I didn't have a chance," replied Leszek, "But if you didn't finish your attack, I would have. I was convinced that he was a Junkers. They look damned alike, especially in the late evening light!"

Leszek tried to comfort the despondent Marian who was unable to recover after his unfortunate "victory," clapping him on the shoulder and saying:

"I wouldn't want to have to come up against you."

This helped Marian a little, but he still sighed dolefully:

"At least they don't know who attacked them ... I wouldn't be able to face them otherwise."

Marian still had to write one more report, while the rest of the pilots broke up to help their mechanics in protecting and hiding the planes for the night.

Fog and silence had descended on the airfield by the time we returned to our quarters.

The car rolled along slowly, with its headlights out, over the bumpy field road.

"Smoke?" Marian turned to me offering a cigarette. "You know I can't stop thinking about Władek. What a great friend and pilot he was! I still can't believe he's dead. One fatal mission, his first and last."

We were lost in our thoughts. War really doesn't change much about a pilot's career. In peacetime even the most uncomplicated flight may have the same tragic end. There is only one real difference: enemy fire, but this only increases the danger.

After a while the driver came to an abrupt stop and we poured out of the vehicle.

In an instant buckets of cold water were snatched up, and everyone had a bath in the school's backyard, where we were staying for the time being. The water had a salutary effect; we all felt better. After supper we went to our rooms. I had already fallen asleep when I felt a sudden, stabbing pain in my stomach that awakened me. I reached up to grab Paweł's leg. He had climbed up on top of me to get to the window.

"They're bombing Toruń!"

Everyone jumped to their feet.

"Certainly the airfield," said someone perceptively, "and the railway loading platform! A general evacuation was begun there this evening. Apparently German intelligence sources have provided precise information."

Through the open window in the dead of night, we could hear the dull thud of explosions and the drone of planes. Without any opposition—just like in the training exercises—the Germans worked their target over.

"Even at night they don't give us any rest," grumbled Karol half asleep.

"They pound us however they want and whenever they want. Just imagine what must be going on at the front?"

"We are strong, united, and . . . ready," someone said.

The intensity of the sound of the bombardment gradually abated. From then on, only sporadically, could we hear the characteristic groan of the engines of individual planes flying in the area. We went to sleep.

Chapter Six

In a Double Pincer

THE SKY WAS CALM AND FILLED WITH THE MORNING DAMP. BELOW, THE ground exhibited all the colors of the rainbow in the radiance of the rising sun. I could see nature slowly coming to life. Smoke from the chimneys lazily floated over the fields, while the Vistula flowed on in the morning mist.

My engine rumbled evenly as my plane, slightly shaking, gained altitude. I was with Wejwer on patrol in the Chełmża–Chełmno–Świecie–Grudziądz region. My altimeter read 800 meters. To guarantee better observation I kept below the clouds.

I switched on my radio.

"Hello! Hello!" I said.

"No answer, it's conked out again," I thought to myself.

I looked around for my wingman whom I couldn't find on my left or on my right. Wejwer, it seems, had fallen back on my tail. I waved my wings trying to get him to realize that he had to return to the proper position. He then moved up alongside me, after which I nodded my head. We were safe now from surprise because we could observe for each other.

Flying toward Chełmża I changed course in a more southerly direction, toward Chełmno–Świecie. On my right I noticed in the distance a silhouette, which I couldn't quite make out, also flying in a southerly direction. I made an immediate turn and, switching on my booster, I tried to intercept its path.

I arrived a little high among the broken clouds. After having gotten a little closer, though, I could see it was a Dornier-215. I dipped down trying to hide myself from its crew against the background of the terrain, and continued on in this way before finding a suitable position to attack. The Dornier flew on calmly at its cruising speed, not seeing me at all. My airspeed indicator read 300 km/hr.

"I hope he doesn't see me till the last instant," I thought to myself. I was right underneath him. Altitude was the only thing separating us. Above me glistened the plane's light blue underside. I suddenly pulled back on the stick and attacked his blind spot, almost perpendicularly. Then I jumped back about 50 meters under his tail. A brief moment for aiming, and I pulled the trigger.

Nothing!

Violently, nervously I pulled the trigger again several times—without any effect. I held my position, however, because I could see there was no gunner in the plane's rear turret. I pulled back the bolt, re-arming both guns, and, aiming, pulled the trigger again. Again nothing. "They're jammed," I thought to myself, and waved my wings to yield my position to my wingman. We had to change places. I looked to my side and rear, but Wejwer was nowhere to be found. At that moment the Dornier realized what was happening and opened fire on me, forcing me to break off the attack. I swung a loop and dove down. While diving I could see that the Dornier's engines were spewing smoke, which was a clear indication that its pilot had pushed the throttle ahead. I finally pulled up, and after a while I could see the Dornier disappear into a thick bank of clouds. I looked around in search of Wejwer. He was gone without a trace. I couldn't contain my anger because—working to clear the guns—I was unable to change the position of the damned bolt.

Giving up, I finally flew off in the direction of the assigned region of patrol, watching carefully so that I wouldn't become a victim of German fighters.

In the region of Grudziądz, I was driven off by a flurry of fire from German artillery. On the way home, while I was flying low over friendly territory, I also came under heavy machine-gun fire from our own infantry—which wasn't an isolated case in the campaign. Everyone shot at us: friend and foe. Very often friendly fire was more deadly. Many of our front-line troops couldn't distinguish between the silhouettes of their own planes and those of the enemy. They thought every plane was German. The news had even been spread that the Germans painted our insignia on their own planes, which wasn't true. Substandard military intelligence was one thing in peacetime, but it bore tragic fruit in time of war. Fear of air attacks created an atmosphere in which all planes were shot at, regardless of their insignia.

After landing I was ready to tear into Wejwer, but I quickly composed myself. The squadron commander himself calmed me down. It appeared that I wasn't entirely correct to suspect him of cowardice and flight. His plane had broken down, and it was only due to his skill as a pilot that he was able to make it back at all. This fact was indisputable because he was backed up in this matter by the mechanics, who were the least inclined to forgive cowardice.

The mechanics didn't like it when a pilot griped about his plane without reason. They were the first to denounce anyone who, under the pretext of defects in his plane, returned from a mission ahead of time. So if the mechanics took a pilot's side, then it was conclusive proof that he was not at fault. And we had good and honest mechanics. A mutual trust constituted the foundation of our unity and strength.

I therefore withdrew my unjustified attacks on him. I only regretted the bad luck that prevented us from exploiting a rare opportunity.

The armorers worked very hard to remove the jam from my guns. They assured me that it would have been impossible for me to have gotten them to work while I was in flight. The cause of the jam was an old one: stale ammunition. In entering the chamber the cartridge cracked, which resulted in a splinter and the bolt locked in the open position. So the squadron commander recommended that the armorers closely examine the ammunition and, when loading belts, to remove defective rounds.

Mirek turned to Paweł and asked for a map, and spread it out on the ground. We had received new orders. Paweł was to lead Karol and me on an assignment to escort light bombers on an attack on the German airfield at Piła [Schneidemühl]. The bombers were to arrive, circle the field, and wait until we could form up with them. There wasn't much time, so we quickly reviewed the flight course and ran to our planes to await the arrival of the bombers. We shook hands and wished each other luck, climbed into our planes, and waited for the bombers. Time began to drag on. The rendezvous time had already passed, and the bombers were nowhere to be found. Discouraged, we began to discuss the causes for the delay, when Mirek suddenly told us to shut up, listen, and look to the northwest.

"It's them," he shouted, pointing in their direction, "they're coming, start your engines!"

Paweł's and Karol's planes began to warm up.

"Dammit!" I cursed. My engine choked, coughed, and spurt fire out the exhaust, together with puffs of white smoke. But it stubbornly refused to turn over.

"Engine off, full throttle!" shouted the mechanic.

"Engine off, full throttle," I repeated.

The mechanic grabbed the propeller and began to turn it to clear the cylinders.

"Take off!" shouted Mirek to Paweł and Karol, pointing to a German plane, which looked like a Dornier-215, flying by. The German disappeared behind the trees while both Jedenatkas dashed along the green field. I, however, continued to work with the mechanics for a little while longer on my choked engine until it finally roared to life. I wiped the sweat from my face and called to Mirek:

"Where are they?"

"In the direction of Złotoria!" he replied.

I tore off in that direction, climbing at a steep angle. From a distance I could recognize the silhouettes of three planes: a large one—a Dornier, and two smaller planes behind him at a safe distance. The German was being chased in a southerly direction. At an altitude of 1,500 meters I leveled off, but—seeing that I was hopelessly far from the Dornier—I decided to circle above the airfield and observe him.

Somewhere above the bend in the Vistula, around Złotoria, the Dornier changed its direction, making a large turn while maintaining a safe distance between itself and the pursuing Jedenastkas, finally heading off due north—straight for me. I began to maneuver, dipping down to position myself for a frontal attack. Neither of the pursuing Jedenastkas were able to close in on the Dornier, and thus remained behind it. Hurriedly I reloaded my guns and—having learned from experience—tested the bolt. The distance between us decreased. We were coming right at each other. The Dornier grew in my gun sight. We opened fire on each other almost simultaneously, and our gunfire crisscrossed. I kept my finger on the trigger, holding fire till I had to pull away to avoid hitting him. A thick, black smoke began to pour out of the Dornier's right engine. Then, instead of turning into a dive, against all logic, I shot up in a chandelle, at the same time rolling over on my back to gain speed and re-position myself to attack the Dornier from behind. The Dornier went into a shallow dive, firing constantly from his gun turret. I dove behind him, and still being in a good position, fired three short bursts after which the gun turret stopped firing. The Dornier, although flying on only one engine, continued to pull away from me. I followed him down to ground level as the distance between us grew to 700 meters.

The German was able to save himself through speed and by flying at ground level, escaping in the direction of Bydgoszcz. He fanned his right propeller, but black smoke, nonetheless, traced his path. Near Solec I broke off the pursuit because I didn't have a chance of catching him. Despite a damaged engine the Dornier was still faster than my Jedenastka.

Ahead of me I could see Paweł and Karol, who, upon watching my actions and final resignation, broke off their chase too. A little while later we all landed together. When we were on the ground I straightened Mirek out. He had watched the combat from below and had thought that I had shot the Dornier down. From these encounters we realized that the most effective method of attack in our case—where the enemy was twice as fast as we—was a frontal attack. This was the only method that promised success. Attack from behind, which has always been the standard method in air combat, was possible for us only in cases of surprise or when we enjoyed a significant altitude advantage over some of the enemy's slower planes. Pursuit was not decisive; it merely wasted fuel and effort. If the Germans didn't want to fight, they could easily fly off and increase the distance between us.

Later on we discovered that the bombing attack on Piła was recalled because of unfavorable atmospheric conditions. The "obstacle" turned out to be high cloud cover. I have to say that those who took part in this sole planned operation over German soil in September 1939 were very lucky. This operation was unsuccessful only because of a lack of intelligence and knowledge of the decisive factors. The question remains, however, what might have happened to the squadron of bombers (nine planes) and its escort trio if these beneficial clouds were not such an important obstacle for our superiors? I dare say it would have taken a miracle to save even a few of us; but even this is doubtful. The only thing we could have done under these conditions, even with complete cloud cover, was to execute the mission. Only the clouds were able to save us from certain destruction. Only they would be able to protect us from the German defense, which was very strong. Yesterday a blunder—the attack on the armored column—cost the lives of three pilots. Today inefficiency and lack of intelligence saved thirty human beings. Once again war revealed itself to be a lottery in which sometimes one tragically loses, and sometimes wins. This time luck was on our side.

We had just about finished our conversations about the events of the past two days when Sergeant Wruś appeared, took me by the arm, and without saying a word, led me over toward the trees. I could immediately see what he was up to: He had set out a spread for me. Wruś, like a caring mother, always tried to get me to eat when I wasn't doing anything.

Sergeant Wruś was the chief mechanic in our squadron. Young, but already an experienced specialist, full of energy and friendliness, he had acquired an exceptional reputation among his subordinates and all the squadron's officers. He was our oracle in technical matters and—I have to say—was never wrong. He educated his subordinates wisely. Sergeant Wruś well knew that the pilot's life depended on the conscientiousness of his mechanics, and he instilled this principle in his subordinates. Later in the war Wruś found himself in England where he was chief mechanic in one of the heavy bomber squadrons. When the unit was reequipped with Lancasters, a heavy four-engine bomber, the English eliminated the position of the second pilot, replacing it with a mechanic/gunner. Thereupon Wruś volunteered to fly. He was killed during one of the many raids over Germany.

At three o'clock the squadron commander called us in to a briefing. Captain Leśniewski designated Lieutenant Zieliński commander. Our mission was to sweep the Chełmża–Chełmno–Grudziądz–Łasin region. We were to fly at an altitude of 1,500 to 2,000 meters. Zieliński, embarrassed by the confidence shown in him, and twitching his left eyelid that had been injured in an accident, requested to be relieved of command. Finally everyone acknowledged that since I was particularly lucky it would be best if I were made commander, which would supposedly guarantee the success of the mission. Everyone laughed at such arguments, but Captain Leśniewski recommended that I assume command of the two flights anyway. I thought that it would be nice if their predictions about my luck came true, and after having spoken to the assigned pilots I briefly discussed the mission.

We had been in the air for half an hour and had not encountered any enemy planes. Around Chełmża I turned north in the direction of Chełmno. From a distance I could see the dark silhouette of a Henschel-126 flying in a southerly direction toward Bydgoszcz. He crossed the Vistula and, not seeing us, continued on the same course. I turned left and catching up with Paweł and Karol from behind signaled to them the plane below us in the distance. They nodded acknowledgment. Paweł immediately banked and dropped down. He was followed by Corporal Klein from the other flight. The German, however, spotted the attacking planes and, still being at a safe distance, turned abruptly to the left and escaped into a high bank of cumulus clouds. He was followed at about 600 to 700 meters by Paweł and Klein. I remained at the same altitude however. Above me I could see Zieliński and Corporal Łysek. I decided not to participate in the pursuit, but to hang back and cut off any escape route for the returning plane.

The Henschel still had some distance to traverse before he could reach the safety of the clouds, where he was sure he would be able to find protection from the pursuing planes. To my surprise he didn't fly into them, but—skating alongside them—wheeled around to the left. I could see the Jedenastkas catch up with him and hang on his tail, and then I lost complete sight of them. The clouds got in the way.

Karol and I turned around to the northern side of the clouds, at a safe distance, waiting for the enemy to exit from them or from behind them. The only recourse for the German would be to separate himself from the pursuing planes and head north for friendly territory. I knew that if both Jedenastkas didn't catch up with him, we would.

A little while later I could see a dark silhouette coming toward us. I quickly dropped down, signaling to Karol at the same time to keep closer on my tail. This would give him a better attack position if the German was able to escape me. Zieliński in the meantime waited above to attack the fleeing plane from the advantage of higher altitude. Behind the Henschel, at a distance of about 300 meters, I could see both Jedenastkas tenaciously pursuing him. The German was thus in a double vise. In his position there was nothing he could do except fight.

I attacked head-on at the same altitude as he. After a second burst from a distance of less than 100 meters, the German plane caught fire and tumbled down as I dodged him. Not wanting to expose myself to his observer's fire, I pulled up and hung above him. I could see something pop out of the burning, diving plane, and shortly thereafter I could see the parachute's white canopy. I spiraled down following the outcome of the encounter. A column of fire shot up as the plane crashed into the ground, killing the other member of the plane's crew.

Half a kilometer in the distance I could see recurrent zigzags of trench lines winding from west to east. I remained aloft alone together with the slowly descending German. There were no planes around. All the other Jedenastkas had disappeared. I circled the parachute as it came down. The German's face was covered with blood, but he didn't act as if he was seriously wounded.

Finally he reached the ground, upsetting a bunch of goats who kicked up a cloud of dust while the parachute's white canopy settled on the gray turf. Once on the ground the German immediately got up, freed himself from his parachute, and began to run in the direction of a nearby wood, about 300 meters away from our defensive lines. Once again it fell to me to capture him. Only this time I decided to do it from the air.

I banked my plane into a shallow dive and fired a short burst in front of the running German. He fell to the ground. I then turned back on him and saw that he had gotten up and had started to run toward the wood again. "So that's your game"—I thought to myself. I repeated my maneuver, this time firing much closer at him, careful as before not to hit him. It was only after the third time that the German knelt on the ground and waved a white flag. I dipped my wing to acknowledge that I accepted his surrender.

I circled over him until four of our infantrymen were able to come over and take him prisoner. I escorted all of them to our line of trenches. After a few aerobatics above the enthusiastic soldiers, who threw their caps and helmets into the air, I took off in a northerly direction.

Although I was alone I still had some fuel and ammunition, so I decided to look for targets of opportunity and headed off for my assigned area of patrol. Over the Vistula something caught my eye. I made a half-turn, heading the plane in the opposite direction. No doubt about it: There was a lone Henschel-126 ahead, flying below me at an altitude of about 800 meters. He was probably returning from a reconnaissance mission to his base in Pomerania.

Enjoying a 1,000-meter altitude advantage, I was sure that I would have enough speed to catch him. Completely hidden in the sun, I waited for my victim. He wouldn't be able to see me until it was too late. When the Henschel got to the Vistula, I found myself directly over him. I made a turn and had him in my gun sight. I positioned myself for a dive, waiting for the appropriate situation to fire on him from the smallest angle of attack. I was almost in the ideal position. Another moment and I'll open fire . . .

Unexpectedly, the German pulled up suddenly, making it impossible for me to fire at him. The chaotic fire from the Henschel's observer, accompanying this maneuver however, proved that both flyers had seen me earlier. "Aha. . . ." The pilot had nervously played possum, and only at the last instant reacted with this splendid maneuver, making it impossible for me to shoot at him. This undoubtedly was an excellent pilot.

I followed his maneuver, pulling even closer to him. However, when I approached to attack, the pilot pulled up again and eluded my gun sight.

"He's beginning to lead me down the garden path," I thought to myself. "I'd better watch out, this won't be an easy fight."

The combat took place beside a bridge over the Vistula. We changed position, and both planes hung inverted in the air for a while, after which we went into a nose-dive. After this last maneuver I was able to get closer on his tail, so close that I got caught in his prop-wash. The German fought beautifully in the vertical; I was amazed by his control and perfect sense of timing, which at the decisive moment accurately anticipated my own thoughts and with sudden maneuvers eluded my fire. I couldn't even draw a bead on him, not to mention delay any corrections.

The enemy observer didn't have a chance to fire effectively on me, however. Sudden changes and rapid maneuvers nearly paralyzed him. Centrifugal force must have pushed him into his seat. Under such circumstances it must have taken no small force for him to make even the slightest arm movement. Not threatened by the observer's fire, I was able to hang tenaciously on the plane's tail and patiently wait for the right moment or a pilot error. One loop turned into an Immelmann turn, and again the plane went into a nose-dive only to extend this into a beautiful loop. I was often seized by an overwhelming desire to pull the trigger, but stopped myself, knowing that I had to conserve my ammunition, of which I had precious little.

I learned patience. I didn't let him get more than 50–70 meters away from me at any time. I had to hold out. I knew that this carousel ride couldn't go on forever, and that the German would have to level off.

The German was well aware of this too. I guessed he was returning from a reconnaissance flight, perhaps even a distant one. A plane's fuel supply decreases rapidly during dogfights at full speed. Each new maneuver reduces the possibility of continuing such defensive combat. He would have to level off sometime. He knew that his life was at stake.

Out of an extended chandelle the plane suddenly rolled over, sending it into a chaotic spin. At first I didn't understand this strange and drastic maneuver. I didn't suspect that he performed this last, wild figure to escape by flying at ground level. I hung almost on his heels, holding myself somewhat beneath his tail in a frantic, inverted dive. Below us was a tract of the Vistula. We were tied together as if by an invisible chain as my speed grew rapidly and the controls stiffened. With difficulty, holding the stick with both hands, I aimed my gun sight at the fuselage of the enemy plane and held him there.

I pulled the trigger.

Just at that moment the German pulled his plane out of the dive, trailing condensation from the tips of his wings. Maintaining pursuit, I pulled up at the same time and sent a second burst in front of the Henschel's nose. The German clung to the ground and headed in the direction of the Koronowo woods.

I was furious with myself that, after two bursts that seemed to hit the plane, nothing happened. True, the observer didn't return fire, but the plane kept on going—and by flying at ground level I couldn't draw a bead on him. So I jumped up a little higher and, waiting to make a correction, I was about to fire off one more burst when I could see a dark trail of smoke coming from the enemy plane's engine. At that moment the distance between us began to decrease rapidly.

"Finally I've got him," I thought to myself with a feeling of vindictive satisfaction. "It was only because of the speed acquired during the dive that he was able to fly for such a distance."

From close in I fired a final short burst directly into the Henschel's fuselage and jumped aside. A cloud of smoke engulfed the entire plane. Its momentum carried it over a ravine, and it crashed at the edge of the woods and exploded. Bits of metal and wood were thrown into the air by the force of the explosion. I was relieved to see that the fire didn't spread and threaten the woods.

I headed back to base, flying along the Vistula. Around Solec I saw a plane flying in a southerly direction at my altitude. At first I thought it was one of our planes. But as I approached it "our plane" took on an entirely different appearance. The similarity between the Jedenastkas and the Henschel-126 was considerable, and you had to get close to tell the difference.

"What a day," I thought. "Three enemy planes in such a short time. How many got away undetected and scot-free at the same time?!" The

Germans had to carry out intensive reconnaissance in this sector, keeping constant sight of our ground forces.

When I got to about 250 meters of him at ground level, the Henschel made a sharp turn to the right. At the same time the enemy observer opened fire. By turning on him I was able to get a little closer, and I pulled the trigger. My guns hesitated and fired off one, maybe two shots. I immediately looked at the bolts. They were in the correct position, so the cause had to be a lack of ammunition. I jumped aside and, for some time still, pretended to pursue him to drive the German off from his intended reconnaissance work. He took off for the Vaterland as fast as his engine could take him.

When I finally landed, my entire flight had already returned. After the first clash Lieutenant Zieliński had flown off with Łysek toward Łasin–Grudziądz. They too shot down a Henschel-126 after a brief encounter.

"Good work!" Zieliński told me. "The one that bailed out, did you capture him? Did you have to land?" he snickered.

Everyone accepted the wisecrack with a laugh.

"Why'd you leave me?" I asked Paweł. "Were you out of fuel or ammunition? Perhaps you were in a hurry to get home? You chicken! We certainly would have gotten one more. If you were out of ammunition, I could understand."

Paweł acknowledged his mistake.

"I'm sorry, Stasiu, I won't make the same mistake again. Maybe tomorrow I'll get a chance to make it up to you. But you have the damnedest luck! From now on I'm flying with you. Mirek," he said, "assign me as his permanent wingman, you won't be disappointed!"

The squadron commander, satisfied with the day's events, shook his hand.

"Well, men, drive over to Franie Skiba to write your reports, we don't have much time!"

Just then the two remaining planes from the 141st Squadron returned to base without having encountered any enemy planes.

That evening in the barn, in the presence of the entire group, by the light of stable lamps, the officer of the day, Lieutenant Czapiewski, read out the units' orders of the day. "The commander of air operations for the Pomorze army designates Captain Tadeusz Rolski group commander, and Lieutenant Marian Pisarek to command of the 141st Squadron . . .

". . . Point three:

"In connection with actions carried out by the fighter group—Toruń on the 2nd of September 1939 I commend the unit's entire complement.

"Congratulations to the heroic group!

"This was signed: Army and Air Force Commander in the name of the Commander in Chief."

"Please be seated," said Lieutenant Czapiewski solemnly in conclusion.

In returning to our quarters we congratulated Tadeusz and Marian on their promotions. Both of them, however, received their distinctions without enthusiasm, even coolly because it signified an exchange of post with someone who yesterday had been alive: with someone who had been a best friend. In Captain Laskowski we lost an excellent commander who was able to foresee the burden that would fall on our shoulders, how air combat would unfold, and how we would have to prepare for it. He was a superb air tactician. His ideas were reflected in later air actions in the war. The concept of fighters fighting in groups had its origin in our group with Captain Laskowski. We were the first to rehearse encounters over the Toruń airfield, practicing frontal attacks in large groups in close order. Captain Laskowski emphasized the improvement of the method of attack, fighting in groups, rapid orientation as well as the refinement of firing in flight from different positions and directions, which became the foundation of fighter pilot combat preparation and combat value.

In the evening after supper, the group commander spread out a map in front of himself, and for some time surveyed things. Finally, raising his head, he looked at us, and called for Pisarek, Zieliński, and me.

"Tomorrow starting at dawn we will reconnoiter this sector," which he outlined with a pencil on the map. "The purpose of this mission is to provide our commander with precise information on large enemy movements. This will be a continuous action. Planes will take off in succession so that they will overlap. There are to be no gaps in our observations. The order of takeoff will be the following: Skalski, Zieliński, Pisarek.

I frowned at the order, and Tadeusz looked at me with surprise.

"What's bothering you?" he asked.

"These early hours annoy me. There's nothing worse than to interrupt a good night's sleep!" I answered.

"Then you better ask the Germans to delay their actions to a more suitable hour, when you've awakened!" he replied.

"I'm interested in knowing what the light bombers and observer planes are doing that we have to take on so many reconnaissance missions?" asked Zieliński. "After all, this is their work, not ours."

"They're flying too," answered Tadeusz, "only, unfortunately, they have suffered many losses. Especially the observer planes. The Germans shoot them down like pigeons. Our planes are faster and more agile, and so it's much easier for us to fly over enemy territory. At the present moment reconnaissance is our most important mission. Our army is in great danger of being outflanked, and so we have to make every effort to observe all enemy movements. The deep incursion of advanced armored units on our rear might cause the main part of our army to be cut off from supplies. The consequences of that are unthinkable! So our mission has great significance. We can't allow this kind of surprise to occur. We have to permit our army to make the proper defensive actions in time."

The briefing ended.

The third night of the war had fallen. Darkness enveloped the tormented land—ravaged by artillery shells and bombs.

From the very beginning of the conflict, the entire border had endured the fire of furious combat. The Germans, attacking with surprise, had, in the course of three days, won the battle along the entire frontier and expanded their Blitzkrieg with the help of mechanized-armored penetrations, supported by a powerful air force. With their obstructions and defensive fortifications in ruins, Polish units were often forced into chaotic retreat.

In the north, from western Pomerania, the army of General von Kluge attacked from west to east and, cutting us off from the sea into the Chojnice–Grudziądz sector, turned quickly south to protect the right flank of the army attacking from eastern Prussia in the direction of Narew–Modlin. Under the blows of the armies of Generals Küchler and Reichenau, attacking from the region of Wrocław [Breslau] and Kluczbork [Kreuzburg], General Szylling's Kraków army suffered a major defeat. Upper Silesia and the southern part of the Kraków province fell to the enemy, and with them the industries of Silesia.

A dangerous and powerful wedge had been driven into the Polish defensive lines in the Radom region. From Czechoslovakia in the south, an attack was developed through the mountain passes. Only General Kutrzeba's Poznań Army held its original position.

A ring of steel inexorably began to close around the entire country. The German army, well armed, and with a speed hitherto unknown in warfare, pushed decisively forward, destroying all resistance. Under incessant bombing by the Luftwaffe, which, it must be said, received no resistance in the air, the entire region of the immediate rear and remote bases of supplies began to sink into chaos. Communication and transport faced complete disorganization and catastrophe.

We tried to do everything in our power to resist the enemy.

CHAPTER SEVEN

The Air Battle over Poczałkowo

IT WAS ALMOST MIDDAY WHEN, RETURNING FROM A RECONNAISSANCE mission, I landed at the field base. After switching off my engine, I climbed out of my plane and, from behind the trees, I could hear the roar of unfamiliar engines. Suddenly over the airfield, at an altitude of about 2,000 meters, appeared a Dornier-215, which, after making a wide turn over the field, flew off in a northwesterly direction. This was already the second time this same morning that we had seen a German plane over the field. He was probably looking for our base. And so I had hardly been able to report the course of my reconnaissance mission, providing the enemy's position as well as his movements, before the commander ordered the immediate evacuation of the group. Believing the Germans would soon bomb the field, he decided to move to another one a few kilometers to the northwest. Shortly thereafter a truck of mechanics took off for the new location in order to be able to receive the planes when they arrived. Within an hour of the command to move, the group left the airfield, while Lieutenant Pisarek received an order to carry out a mission and land at the new field. Only a motorcyclist remained. He was to bring Zieliński back to us after the latter had landed from the mission he was already on.

We landed on a nice, hard field adjoined by a large group of trees. The planes quickly disappeared into the shade at the end of the woods, hastily camouflaged by the mechanics. The field was deserted, but the woods were alive with the buzz of human voices as we organized a new encampment.

At first we were happy with the change because the new field was longer than the old one and exceptionally flat. But the woods, or rather what we found within them, made us change our minds. Deeper within, in a large open area, lay a collection of gray, massive bombs scattered about haphazardly. There were enough of them to equip a light bomber for a year of intensive activity. We were dismayed. The prospect of staying in this location did not fill us with optimism. A few well-placed bombs and our entire group would be wiped out. Captain Rolski therefore issued the order to be very careful. He had concluded that any further stay here would only end disastrously.

"We've jumped from the frying pan into the fire," said Mirek, looking with very reserved amusement on the sleek shapes of the 100-kilogram bombs. "Better that we get out of here, Tadziu, while we still have the chance."

The characteristic sound of a Jedenstaka flying nearby brought us out of the woods.

"The Germans are already in Solec," announced Zieliński. "Outside of that I didn't see any movements in the area, though the artillery scared me a little."

"If you want to be scared even more, take a look in the woods," said Mirek.

"Marian's back!" shouted someone, pointing to the approach of a low-flying plane. But along with the sound of the approaching Jedenas-tka we could also hear in the distance the sullen murmur of large planes.

Germans were flying somewhere nearby!

We started to listen intently. The groan of the engines came ever closer. They were coming from the west, and the woods would protect us only on one side from observation. In the meantime Marian had circled and was making his landing approach.

"Dammit, they're coming this way!" fretted Tadeusz. "He had to choose this moment to land!"

Everyone made a commotion, as if trying to do something to prevent the unfortunate landing. But it was already too late. Marian had touched down and taxied over toward us, kicking up a trail of dust behind him. At the same time three enemy planes, flying in tight formation, appeared over the edge of the woods. Dornier-17s passed by majestically at an altitude of 2,500 meters.

"Well, if they unload now," uttered Zieliński almost in a whisper, "then . . ."

After a moment of intense anticipation, however, the danger passed. The Germans just flew off.

"They didn't notice Marian's landing," remarked Mirek in amazement.

We quickly brought his plane into the bushes. Someone suggested that we take off. But that idea was quickly stifled by the sight of a 180-degree turn by the bombers. At least we had moved ourselves farther away from the bomb dump. The Germans straightened out and once again came at us in formation. Their behavior was—to put it mildly—suspicious. It seemed as if they were scrupulously looking for something, maneuvering a little before descending for a closer look. In silence we watched the approaching planes. There was nothing left to do but hug the ground and wait for the first bombs to fall.

"I guess today they pound us!" grumbled Karol lying on his back, intently observing the Dorniers. "Well, come on, dammit, how long do you intend to keep us waiting!"

"Wouldn't you rather be up there, than lying here like a defenseless lump?" whispered someone unknowingly.

"They're on top of us!" I blurted out with bated breath. We could see their ominous shadows, which passed over the airfield, reached the edge of the woods, and skipped over the treetops. Their engines roared full throttle while their white bellies hung over us . . .

And then they passed by.

"Now you can drop your bombs!" someone shouted.

We could hear the roar of their engines slowly recede into the distance.

"Don't unload the remaining trucks! Reload all the unloaded equipment quickly!" ordered the group commander. "We're changing airfields!"

After a brief conference with the commanders, one of the numerous airfields in the network was selected—a field near the estate of Poczał-kowo, a little to the southwest. We had to leave hastily from the area, which was becoming increasingly threatened by enemy visits. This time they didn't find us. Their target had probably been our former airfield in Markowo, and it was only by accident that they didn't discover us when Pisarek landed. We could expect that they wouldn't forget us, though. The presence of the bomb dump created an additional, particularly threatening, danger.

We were to take off first with the squadron commander as a lead party to organize the departure, and then receive the rest when they landed in Początkowo.

After landing on the bumpy field next to the estate's park, we placed the planes in the shade of the trees. Obstacles on the ground were marked out with red flags, and twenty minutes later, in equal intervals, the remaining flights landed and were camouflaged. We awaited only the ground crews. In the meantime, the group commander left in a car for army headquarters in Toruń.

Across the field we could see an unidentifiable group of people approaching.

"They look like soldiers," said Paweł, "but whose uniform. . . ."

The newcomers were stragglers from a division fighting at Chojnice—with a few rifles, exhausted, a few lightly wounded, the majority without anything on their heads, some in helmets and civilian trousers. From what they told us we learned that the 18th Regiment of the Grudziądz light cavalry no longer existed. They had been destroyed by tanks at the battle of Chojnice. Their own division had been destroyed on the first day, and they had been able to force their way through the German encirclement by staying off the roads and walking in a southeasterly direction. They had stopped only because they had encountered us, happy that they had reached their own troops. We couldn't understand why they hadn't seen any of our army on their march.

Since it wasn't yet time to eat, we sent them on to the barn to get a little sleep, proposing at the same time that they remain with us until we met the nearest infantry unit. They greeted this proposition with gratitude.

"It's good if we can keep some distance between us and the Germans. If you remain here, you'll end up like us," they said.

"That's true," said Paweł. "It would be something if the Germans could catch us all together."

These depressing thoughts were interrupted by the arrival of a friendly reporter who invited us to breakfast at the residence of a local priest. Mirek magnanimously granted us a pass for the hour, and a few minutes later we were seated at our guest's table eating and drinking, in no time recalling the actions of the last few days. The hour flew by in an instant. We drank a parting toast to our host, and in the open doors of the residence the old priest bid us farewell with his blessing.

Upon our return Mirek noticed that we were in good spirits.

"The breakfast, I see, must have gone well . . ."

"It was too short, too short," replied Karol.

Later that day we were kidding around when a few of the pilots came out of the park into the open, looking to the northwest part of the sky. There was an increasingly loud murmur coming from that direction. A little while later we could see the dots of an enemy formation looming on the misty horizon.

"Mirek!" shouted Marian, "there's still time to go after them, let's try . . ."

"Sonofabitch!" Mirek lost his temper. "I see them too and I'll be damned! But I can't give the order without Tadeusz's okay! He told me not to send up any planes until he got back—except Zieliński for reconnaissance."

It was an expedition of bombers that we had not seen before, more than 50 Junkers-87s, Dornier-17s, and Messerschmitt-109s, flying placidly in the direction of Włocławek. After the Germans had flown past, Lieutenant Zieliński's Jedenastka was brought out for his reconnaissance mission, and when he had taken off Karol, Paweł, and I assaulted Mirek with requests to allow us to attack the Germans if they returned by the same route. We were excited, and invigorated by the breakfast, we incessantly pressed for an answer, providing ever new arguments to try to get the commander to change his position. Mirek walked around, struggling with himself. After a little while he decided:

"In case we eventually have to take off, Skalski and Pniak will fly with me, Kogut and Wieprzkowicz with Wilczewski. How many planes do you have ready, Marian?"

"Two," he replied. "I'll fly with Leszek."

"Then we have only eight planes ready? Okay. Make sure all pilots are prepared."

Paweł sat down disheartened when his name wasn't called. Due to seniority he was forced to remain on the ground. Mirek did everything he could to convince him, though, that the alert he ordered didn't hold for the eventual attack on the German formation. He counted on the group commander's return by then, which would free him from making the critical decision.

A half-hour had already passed since we had seen the enemy formation. We started to get impatient, thinking that the Germans had changed their route. But after a while we began to hear a faint buzz of engines. Although the formation was still far away, we could figure out that they were heading straight for us. The sound of their engines grew louder.

"Listen, Mirek!" Marian broke the silence, "There's time if we go now . . ."

Mirek didn't answer.

"Let's go, or else it'll be too late," a few of us said.

Everyone was in a state of excitement. The German planes became bigger, closing in on us. Suddenly, somewhere from behind us came the voice of our technical officer:

"Pilots to your planes, ground personnel to the trenches!"

We burst out laughing at the sight of the frightened Erbart who had given the order. At that point Mirek, cheered by the laughter, called out:

"To your planes!"

In an instant the camouflage fell away from the planes, the engines roared, and the brown noses of the Jedenastkas appeared from under the shady branches of the trees. We took off in flights of threes, climbing rapidly. The Germans flew toward us from our right. At an altitude of 800 meters, we made a sharp turn into them at the moment of attack, completely frustrating their tactical advantage.

From the very beginning the battle created an indescribable confusion. We disappeared into an utter torrent of black crosses. The Junkers and Messerschmitts shot up in chandelles. And their fire! Chaotic, but dangerous.

Rolling over on my back, I dove my plane down onto two Ju-87s who were going straight for Mirek. The second German immediately broke off his attack with a sharp turn to the right, while the first hung tenaciously on Mirek's tail. Only after my second burst, notwithstanding the fire of the rear gunner, did he escape by diving for the ground. I didn't let him get away though, but turned and got him in my gun sight. Two short bursts from an opportune position and the Junkers began to fall apart. He was hit, stopped firing, and began to spiral down. I hung tenaciously on his tail and waited only for the end, which seemed to take ages. The ground came up at a dizzying rate, and yet it was still far away. From the corner of my eye, on the right, I could see an explosion and an enormous column of fire. Somebody bought it—friend or foe? Everything dissolved into one gray mass.

Another instant and the German would crash into the ground. With a strong jerk on the stick I pulled the plane straight up. I went black and pain shot through my head. The dizziness, however, was only very brief. I looked down to make sure the German had crashed.

Impossible! I rolled my plane over violently and dove down. Against all expectation, in an astoundingly simple manner, the enemy had pulled his plane out of its dive and at the last instant saved it from crashing into the ground, raising behind him a cloud of dust. He then took off at ground level.

I bit my lip in anger.

It seemed unbelievable: After all he was too low! In the meantime the pilot, exploiting my error, or rather the slowness of my plane, immediately put a safe distance between us, constantly increasing it.

Although his gunner didn't fire, I continued to pursue the Junkers for a long time, but couldn't squeeze anything more out of my plane to catch up with him. The German did a remarkable job, flying as if he were glued to the ground. He was so low that at times his wheels grazed the ground, kicking up a trail of dust. Now and again he would bounce up over an obstacle and then stick to the ground like a pointer. I had no chance of catching him. But I followed him anyway, marveling at his mastery. Finally I realized I had gone too far, broke off my hopeless pursuit, and headed for home.

I was angry with myself for having made a mistake, but also glad it took a truly superb pilot to cause my error. Too bad that I didn't stick with him all the way down—then our game would have ended differently!

I climbed a little to try to get a better view of the ground. On my right lay Inowrocław, so I made a slight turn. I had to correct my course more to the east. Having established my position I dropped down to fly at ground level, carefully watching the sky above for returning Germans. Soon after, I noticed a single Ju-87 flying alongside me on my left. Far behind was a trio of Messerschmitt-109s coming up on him rapidly. Seeing that they soon passed him by and began to fly off, I decided to attack the Stuka. He flew at cruising speed at an altitude of 400 meters, which made it easier for me to catch him, especially because I still had him in front of me. I was only afraid that the Messerschmitts would return. I maneuvered right down to the ground, wanting to attack undetected. In no time I was right below him, in his blind spot. So I shot up in a chandelle with all the force my engine could manage and, from a distance of 70 meters, fired a long burst directly into his belly. He turned suddenly, but I was already on his tail. Fire from his engine and black smoke made it hard for me to draw a bead on him. I corrected, fired a short burst, and then jumped aside. The German flipped over, and in the next instant tumbled down. The gunner jumped out of the rear cockpit, opening his parachute immediately.

Excited with such an unexpectedly short encounter with the Junkers, and preoccupied with the sight of the enemy plane falling in flames toward the ground, I didn't notice at first the traces of gunfire around my wings. When I finally realized what was happening I wondered: Where's that coming from?

"I'd better get down where it's safe," I thought to myself. I looked to my rear and above. The Messerschmitts had not flown off, but were near . . . too near! They stopped firing for the moment because they were not in a good position. So I grabbed the stick in both hands and, staking everything on one single try, violently turned my plane 180 degrees, pulling it right down on the ground in the completely opposite direction from what was expected. There was no chance of pulling straight away from them. They were twice as fast as I. Only by maneuvering would I be able to save my hide, exploit their mistakes, and create a poor target. Oh, hell! Only one thing could save me: exceptional luck in this exceptionally unequal fight!

I was hardly able to pull myself out from under their fire when they came at me again, staggered one after the other, attacking with lightning speed. Flying at ground level becomes extremely dangerous under these conditions. I had to divide my attention, keeping a constant eye on my attackers and at the same time watching out for obstacles on the ground. After their second attack I had to make a split-second decision concerning the direction of escape: back to our base or somewhere else to avoid betraying our position. The thought that everyone else had already returned and would fall victim to the German fighters prevented me from returning home. Therefore I flew in an easterly direction, keeping far to the right of my own airfield. I watched the Germans in my mirror, at the same time watching ground obstacles out of the corner of my eye.

Suddenly the Messerschmitts disappeared from my mirror. I immediately looked around and saw that they were now in a shallow dive. The distance between us was rapidly decreasing. I pushed the throttle forward with my left hand, squeezing it tightly, very tightly. There was a brief, but agonizing moment of delay. I collected myself, and with all my power curbed my excitement. "Calm down! Calm down!" I kept telling myself.

Not yet . . . they're still too far away . . .

Here! Now! Reactions are faster than thought. I turned inside and under the attacking planes, and their fire passed alongside me.

I saw the trio pass over me after their fruitless attack. But this was only for a brief period. The Germans immediately attacked again with lightning speed, not leaving me a second. Dammit! They didn't want to give me a chance to figure out the direction from which they were going to attack. Burst after burst started to hit my wings and fuselage. Now I wasn't in a position to avoid them. But fortunately they were hitting the least sensitive parts of my plane.

The German pilots, having grasped the futility of the combat so far, changed their tactics and alternated their attacks. I now found myself in an even more perilous situation, one that would require maximum concentration and errorless maneuvering under extremely limited conditions. "So long as I escape their trap," I thought to myself.

Slowly I moved ahead, forced to make constant changes of direction. I maneuvered under a hail of bullets in tight turns close to the ground. Often I made complete circles. I became increasingly exhausted by this hopeless struggle for my life. But I didn't think of giving up yet. "No, no I won't surrender!" I told myself.

The Germans, attacking together in turns, apparently decided to exhaust my energy and, exploiting some error, finish me off. Every moment I was faced with danger from three directions. Constantly I had to watch three sections of the sky and at the proper time parry every attack, and even—to the extent possible—anticipate their moves. One of the Germans flew from my front to my rear in an S-turn, and awaited only the right moment. The second hung on my tail on the right side, while the third attacked from behind from my blind spot. I had only one chance: a right turn to avoid the attack of at least one of my opponents. But how could I do this when, at the same time, I had to avoid an attack from the front that would surely come as soon as I turned?

I deliberately decided to allow an attack from my rear at the safest close distance. I counted on the only trump card I had in this passive defense: my Jedenastka's ability to outturn the Messerschmitts, and the low level at which I would be flying, which would prevent the Germans from making an effective attack.

The attacker on my rear was still too far away . . . I kept watching: 400 . . . 300 . . . 200 . . . meters separated us. It turned out that I had anticipated him. I was already in my right turn and his fire passed me by. Good! I held my turn until I made a complete circle seeing that the German who initially was in front of me had turned his plane to attack. The one on my right, who was watching all this, also didn't wait and rolled his Messerschmitt over, and came at me fast. I didn't see where the third one had gone. I kept in my turn and then quickly turned to my left. My Jedenastka shook for lack of speed, but I had already gained the upper hand and squeezed down closer to the ground. The danger had passed; the Germans weren't even able to fire. Getting in each other's way, they pulled off and fanned out. I took advantage of their confusion to get away from them at least for the moment. But unfortunately, I soon had one on my tail again, while the others hung above. "Have they gone over now to individual attacks?" I thought feverishly, not grasping what they had in mind.

This time one of the Germans tricked me and unexpectedly opened fire from a distance while I quickly ducked. He hit me, but his burst was too short and passed over the rear of my fuselage. I had already dropped down over the Toruń firing range whose hilly terrain helped me. At the same time, however, I had to be even more careful not to hit any obstacles on the ground.

Just as the Germans renewed their attacks, I lost sight of the triangulation tower. To avoid hitting it I quickly turned and fell right into the sights of two of the Messerschmitts. The bullets clinked along my wings like peas poured on a tin roof. Dangerously, I pulled up to impede their line of fire, increasing my angular correction. I was still able to avoid getting hit in a sensitive spot and my engine continued to perform flawlessly.

The Messerschmitts were above me once again, circling like vultures over a carcass, after which they separated into different positions and began to dive straight down on me all at once. I was seized with despair, defenseless against their fury and power.

I assumed a frontal attack as we rapidly closed on each other at different speeds. By now I didn't know what was going on behind me. I had only seconds to focus all my concentration on the Messerschmitt coming at me. I knew he had opened fire from a distance with short bursts because I could see the intermittent sparkle of his fire. But he missed me. I aimed my gun sight at his fire and the silhouette of the Messerschmitt grew. I pulled the trigger . . . a short burst and then . . . silence. The trigger went limp. Out of ammunition!

I didn't have time to do anything. This was the most critical moment. I simply didn't see how I could escape from the concentrated attacks of the Germans. Without thinking I pulled back on the stick with both hands and shot straight up. A moment later I side-slipped and dropped my plane on its nose, changing my direction by 90 degrees. Again I was flying at ground level. The Germans, who were circling me, shot up too and separated into an innocuous fan. "Dammit!" I thought to myself, "when are they going to run out of ammunition? I'm already completely out and didn't hit any of them with my last shots. I didn't even get one of them to break off his attack."

Things then suddenly changed. The Germans stopped attacking and reformed into a tight trio. Are they trying to devise something new against me? No! They're passing over me and leaving me behind. I didn't understand their decision: Why abandon me and take off in a southwesterly direction? After all, their base wasn't in that direction.

I kept a close eye on the Messerschmitts, although they began to distance themselves from me by a wide angle. I quickly saw the reason why they abandoned me, so magnanimously forsaking the conclusion of the long and fruitless pursuit. They decided to make up for their failure with me on another victim. I immediately turned after them to come to the aid of my comrade if only by my presence. I wasn't in a position to take active part in the combat because I had no ammunition, but there's always. . . .

When the Germans attacked, the Jedenastka was flying at about 200 meters. "He's hit!" I shouted, terrified to see the plane spinning out of control. One spiral . . . two . . . suddenly the Jedenastka straightened out, and the pilot, after pulling his plane out of its dive just above the ground, flew off at ground level. "No small piece of flying," I thought with admiration.

The Germans didn't give up, however, but renewed their attack. I went after them at full speed even though I was not in a position to join the fight. Speed, speed, and once again speed—this was our true downfall. Speed is a necessary condition of combat, and a condition that our planes didn't meet.

After a fresh attack, the Jedenastka made a tight turn in my direction. Unfortunately, the pilot, undoubtedly not seeing me, finished his maneuver away from me. This time, however, the Germans didn't attack their victim—apparently they were out of fuel or ammunition. They stopped firing and flew off in a westerly direction.

The fight was over.

Now I could finally relax. But relaxation took its toll: I was completely exhausted. After a few minutes following behind the unknown

Jedenastka, I came upon the airfield at the same time that the apparent "suicide" was landing. I had already recognized Zieliński in the air. As it happened, returning from his reconnaissance mission he ran into the aggressive trio of Messerschmitts.

From afar I could see the vestiges of combat. A Jedenastka lay overturned in a field, and at the end of the airfield a group of people stood around the smoking remnants of a plane. The fragments of the planes, scattered over a wide area, bore witness to the fact that they belonged to the Luftwaffe.

I landed beside the overturned Jedenastka.

The mechanics and pilots shook their heads at the sight of my plane. "Look at all the holes. You were lucky!"

Wruś thoughtfully asked me whether by chance I had not been wounded, since my face was rather pale. Our doctor, also concerned with my appearance, examined me. I shook like jelly, unable to control myself. I had to get my feet on the ground and submit to a lengthy examination. I finally agreed that I might have been wounded. Only I didn't feel any pain, perhaps because of the excitement. All fears, however, turned out to be unfounded, and I was given something to help calm my nerves.

Marian found himself in the same situation. Pale and excited, with shaking hands he lifted a cigarette to his mouth. We tried to laugh, but we couldn't very well. The Germans had surely given us a good beating.

"I got one Ju-87," said Marian, "but then three Messerschmitts jumped me so that it took a miracle to get away from them in one piece. My plane was already shot up pretty bad. Every sharp turn made it shake so violently that I thought it would fall apart at any moment. They worked me over, firing from different directions even when they didn't have a chance of hitting me. They eventually gave up, probably because they were out of ammunition. I couldn't see any other reason. I was lucky, however, that I didn't trip my elevator cable while I was in the air because it had been shot through, and held out on a thin steel thread until I landed, when it broke as my wheels hit the ground. I would have crashed beyond repair if it had broken earlier. The entire time they chased me I was too low to bail out. . . ."

Even Marian's trouser legs had bullet holes in them, although he wasn't hit himself. His plane, on the other hand, was completely destroyed. Only the engine escaped and was still useable.

In the shade of the old, majestically rustling trees of the park, there was pandemonium. In the excitement that still abounded among the participants as well as the observers, the course of the battle was discussed. We gesticulated wildly as pilots often do. Questions and answers flew back and forth. Everyone had something to say; everyone's experiences were different from everyone else's. Everyone wanted to contribute his observations about German tactics as well as his own solutions to future fights. A vivid picture of the battle began to develop out of the chaos of the heated discussion.

The most excited were the witnesses of the battle who were forced to watch it from the ground. They could observe the entire situation from the beginning. And it was where we suffered our first loss: Sergeant Nawrot, chief mechanic of the 141st Squadron, was hit in the head by a stray bullet and killed.

"From the ground it looked fantastic," said Paweł. "I don't regret that I wasn't up there because you had to see the whole picture. No film ever showed anything like it. When you dove into that pile, we couldn't see anything. At first we could only hear the thump of cannon-fire, the crack of machine-gun fire, and the whine of engines at full speed. It looked so bad that I was sure that none of us would come out of that cauldron alive. And then suddenly a Ju-87 popped out of the confusion with a Jedenastka on its tail, followed by a second pair in the same situation tearing like hell straight for the ground. One of the Junkers crashed, shooting up a column of fire and smoke. I thought that the second would meet the same fate when, unexpectedly, the German pulled his plane up, literally cheating the grim reaper. I have to admit that he was an excellent pilot and demonstrated unusual control in deciding on such a dangerous maneuver. The entire formation was routed, though. The Germans scattered, fleeing in different directions individually and in groups. The Jedenastkas started to chase after them until we lost sight," ended Paweł.

Gradually everyone began to feel nervous about the prolonged absence of Mirek, Wacek, and Karol. We continued to hope that they still had enough fuel to get back as we waited.

In the meantime Kogut flipped over while landing in a plane with its tires shot out, and Wieprzkowicz came under fire from a nearby German village when he reached the end of the runway. The "fifth column" was active in this area too. A group of soldiers under the command of Ensign Jaugsch was sent to the village to find the culprits.

Leszek was a little depressed when he returned from inspecting the place where his victim lay. He saw the results of his first victory close up. He was surprised that it only took one short burst:

"I didn't see any indication that I hit him, and yet . . ."

"And yet," continued Zieliński, "the Germans were lacking in something. I think that they lacked combat proficiency. Because, considering today's encounter alone, they ought to have smashed us. But despite their overwhelming superiority in all respects, this didn't happen. And if our three remaining pilots are still lucky enough to return, and have any victories of their own, it will certainly be an outstanding success for us and a powerful proof that we too can cause trouble under these extremely unfavorable conditions. The question, however, still remains—for how long? Our planes are falling apart and there's no chance of replacing them."

Taking advantage of some free time, Zieliński and I took a motorcycle ride over to the Junkers crash site. It was still smoldering and we could still feel the heat from the deep crater. Nothing remained of the plane except for bits of metal torn from the wings that were scattered all over the field. The engine was embedded deep in the ground, burying the crew beneath it. The only trace of human beings we could find as we picked through the ruins was a foot broken off at the ankle as well as a field-cap with the owner's name on it. It was an unpleasant experience. It was then, sobered by these remnants, that Zieliński and I decided to address each other in the familiar form from then on.

Stach Zieliński always impressed us with his exceptional enthusiasm and love of flying. He loved the air force and, although he was a reserve officer, he spent a lot of time with the wing, coming by in a colorful RWD-8 from the nearby estate in Skępe to keep up with his training as a fighter pilot. We became very familiar with him and considered him a longtime member of the group and an excellent and valuable fighter pilot. When the unit was mobilized, he volunteered without being called up and made his RWD-8 available to the army—that's the kind of guy he was.

In the manor-house, where our quarters were, we found the group commander who had just arrived from Toruń. He was quite disturbed about the fate of the pilots who had not yet returned. And as time passed it became more certain that we too had suffered painful losses. Our meager dinner was spent in silence, except for an occasional casual question and answer. While we were sitting at the table in this sullen mood, the door suddenly opened and there stood Wacek Wilczewski, whom we had already buried in our minds, smiling at us. We all leaped to our feet hugging the man we thought dead.

Forcing his way to the table and defending himself against our exuberance, he murmured:

"Enough, enough already. Give me something to eat first, I'm starved!"

Asked what took him so long to get back, he declined to explain, even though we were dying of interest.

"That's a long story!" he exclaimed. "I'll tell you as I eat. . . ."

His appetite was really impressive, shoving everything down as fast as he could. He even swallowed without chewing, scoffing at our gibes from time to time. Finally to our delight he finished, and after having drawn on his cigarette he began to tell his story:

"I'm sure you saw everything, so you already know how the fight with the Germans turned out, and therefore how the situation developed. I won't go over this stuff again. I'll begin with what happened to me. Well, not far from here I was chasing a Junkers-87, not paying attention to my own tail. Suddenly my engine choked, and then a little while later choked again. It was only then that I noticed that someone was shooting at me point-blank. There wasn't time to look around. I tore off, holding my breath as I came into land at a nearby field. My attacker left me alone, however, because it seems that he was himself under attack by a Jedenastka. It was only then that I noticed he was a Messerschmitt-109. The German immediately turned to engage his attacker. I wasn't able to follow the course of the fight completely because it was too far away, but I had the feeling that the Messerschmitt was hit and came down in flames. Then the Jedenastka attacked two other Messerschmitts. I don't know what happened next because I lost sight of them beyond the woods. After landing I began to poke around in my engine, looking for the cause of my problems. Not having any tools I had to use my pocketknife. As you can see, I eventually found the problem and came back. But this is not the end of the story. I would have been here a long time ago if it wasn't for a crazy incident with the police. When, if you please, I had almost finished working on my carburetor, a group of people from a nearby village came running towards me with a policeman leading them. He ran up to me with his pistol drawn and putting it to my head began to talk all sorts of nonsense. Among other things, that I was really a German pilot wearing a Polish uniform. I laughed in response, but this didn't convince him. He only got angry and shouted quite seriously that he would shoot me. And, in addition, the people who had come with him started to become hostile. I tried to explain to him who I was and what happened to me, pointing to my plane. Nothing helped. By this time this hopeless scene had already lasted over an hour. During the entire time I had to stand by my plane with my hands in the air. The policeman who—I could see—was drunk, waved his gun under my nose shouting obstinately that "such scoundrels have to be caught red handed." By now I had lost my sense of humor and had resigned myself to dealing with an idiot because the situation had ceased to be comical. Then by accident the imbecile conducting this examination asked me where I had come from. I answered that I had come from the 4th Air Regiment in Toruń."

"Really?" he replied dubiously. "If you're from the 4th Air Regiment, then you must know its officers."

"Of course, I know them," I said, seeing a chance to extricate myself from this unpleasant situation.

"And," he asked, "do you know Lieutenant Babiański?"

"Of course!"

"Well then, what's his first name?"

Although I hardly knew Babiański, I luckily remembered his first name.

"Tomasz . . . Tomek. He's one of my best friends," I said.

This completely disarmed the policeman, and then I became indignant and intimidating:

"Release me immediately, dammit, I don't have time for your silly games!"

"Please forgive me, lieutenant sir," mumbled the policeman, "but the area is full of 'fifth columnists,' and so . . ."

I didn't waste any more time on him and jumped into my plane. That, gentlemen, was my fight and 'brief captivity.'"

"Some adventure!" said Paweł. "You're lucky that Tomasz likes to have a drink every now and then around these parts. His acquaintance with the policeman was no accident."

After Wacek's return we were a little more at ease, and his story took our minds off our other somber thoughts. Suddenly above our building we could hear the buzz of a Jedenastka flying by.

"The next one's coming!" I shouted as I pointed to the courtyard.

A crippled plane with its wing tip shot off was coming in for a landing. Someone recognized the pilot from afar:

"It's Edek Jankowski!"

We warmly greeted our old buddy on whose return no one had counted. The last time we had seen him was on the 2nd of September before he took off. Due to a lack of fuel he had landed somewhere around Sierpc, where only this morning he had been reached by a ground crew that provisionally repaired his minor problems and filled his plane with fuel. Despite the major damage to his wing—he was missing a good meter off its tip—Edek decided to take off and, flying the plane with both hands despite a decided bank to one side, he luckily reached us.

We got the feeling that he was still in shock from the attack on the armored column. This was a very dangerous sign because it might lead to a complete collapse. A loss of confidence in oneself is the most dangerous condition for a fighter pilot.

The news of our losses only increased his depression, and his face began to twitch nervously. A fear began to appear in his eyes that he couldn't hide with a forced smile. His eyes reflected his true feelings: They were filled with dread. Edek wanted to live at any cost simply because death had come so close to him.

Time—the ultimate judge—showed now that any expectation that there would be additional arrivals from the last sortie was unjustified. The chances that Mirek or Karol would return decreased to almost zero; their fuel must have long since run out. And yet we still waited, deceiving ourselves that they would return. The group commander walked around with a frown on his face, deliberating, considering different possibilities . . . he at least still had hope.

Two planes went out on reconnaissance, and the mechanics worked feverishly on the rest to make them combat-ready after the damage they had received in the recent combat.

Marian suggested that we go out and try to call Jaugsch back in. But no sooner had we started than he answered our call, profoundly convinced that he had received orders to perform some important mission. But his appearance gave us all a laugh. Hung with map-cases, with a formidable pistol slung under his arm, and field glasses, he created the impression of a trapper from the Old West worried about the presence of hostile Indians. He was everywhere, wanting to do everything, trying to be accommodating and obliging to everyone. He was no small source of comfort and delight to us all. He was able to disarm anyone with his naiveté and exceptionally noble character.

With a serious look Marian asked him some casual questions about the recent battle. He immediately lit up, threw his cap on the ground, and began to describe the course of the encounter vividly, waving his hands about to symbolize the most fantastic positions of the planes in the fight. His eyes flashed and his kindly face depicted in succession the feelings of rapture, wonder, terror, and dread. We laughed until we cried. I asked him about the outcome of the action he had to carry out in the nearby German village.

"We didn't find anything," he said. "There were too few of us and we didn't stay long enough. If we want to find anything we'll have to go back and turn the town upside down. I'd bet my ass that those Krauts are armed. And they became so docile when we appeared with guns. They immediately showed respect. I screamed at them a little bit, and before leaving the village I ordered them all into the square and threatened that, if there was one more shot coming from their direction, the village would be cleared and the buildings burned down. Then they started to look at one another. . . ."

Off in the distance on the field road we could see our ambulance driving off in the direction of Toruń. We watched it go until there was nothing left but a cloud of dust. I looked at Marian nonplussed. This was not a good omen. Jaugsch, who had been sent out on a reconnoitering party, returned a little later with no news. Nobody knew where or why the ambulance was going, and we waited impatiently for it to return. About an hour later it returned along the same road, leisurely crawling along in the direction of the manor-house.

"He must be one of ours!" exclaimed Marian. We had arrived as the wounded pilot was being removed from the ambulance . . .

"Mirek!" he screamed, unable to control himself at the sight of the bloodied and burned body. I leaned over the stretcher, but the words stuck in my throat. He looked at me with his gentle eyes.

"Did everyone get back?" he whispered in a strange voice, still concerned about the fate of his subordinates.

"We're all here," I said quietly. "We were waiting only for you. . . ."

I purposely concealed from him that Karol, whom he respected and liked, was still missing. With relief he closed his eyes. The ambulance attendants lifted the stretcher and carried him into the main room. Shortly thereafter the doctor came by. We waited outside in the corridor by the door to be called into the room.

We didn't talk. But from behind the door we could hear Mirek groan as his wounds were being dressed. It frayed our nerves. After about twenty minutes of waiting, which seemed interminably long, the doctor came to the door.

"You may come in now, only please don't tire him with talking too much because he is seriously weakened by loss of blood. Captain, sir," he turned to the group commander, "we should really take Captain Leśniewski to the nearest hospital as soon as possible. He's seriously burned and has a severe gunshot wound to the shoulder. He also needs a blood transfusion."

We sat at the edge of the bed where Mirek lay covered in bandages.

"Feeling better?" asked Tadeusz.

"Much ... ," he said, smiling with obvious effort. "I'm back home ... get any planes?"

"Sure!" replied Tadek. "Marian, Leszek, and Stach each got a Junkers-87. And you, it seems, brought down a Messerschmitt-109, saving Wacek. So he tells us."

"I'm very happy," he said as he looked at Wacek, "that I was able to save you from danger. I thought you were finished and that I would be too late ... "

Wacek began to mutter something about his indebtedness and regret that everything ended the way it did. But Mirek interrupted him:

"Nonsense, it's all in the past!"

We wanted to comply with the doctor's orders, but Mirek protested:

"Don't leave ... I'm feeling better. At least I've forgotten about the pain."

But the spasmodic clenching of his lips belied the fact that it was only with the greatest of effort that he was able to control his pain.

"I'm not dead yet," he suddenly said in an unexpectedly strong voice. "Just wait till I get better, I'll get them for this."

"You'll be back with us in two, three weeks," I interjected. "Did you have a hard time with them?"

"Everything happened so fast," he said. "I didn't have time to think. I had to make split-second decisions. If I had to think it would have been too late. I was following the burning Messerschmitt down and then at low level I was hit somewhere in the area of my shoulder. The same burst also hit my fuel tank, and my plane immediately caught fire. . . ."

Beads of sweat began to appear on his forehead, but he continued to describe his ordeal.

"I wasn't able to bail out ... too low. All I could do was to push the lever forward and jettison the burning fuel tank. The Germans never stopped firing at me, even after I had landed on this lousy, bumpy field.

I couldn't even see where I had landed. I felt dizzy, and an immense pain seized my entire body. I landed half-conscious . . . I must have hit something, though, because my undercarriage shattered and my plane flipped over. I struggled in the cockpit and for a little while—I don't even know for how long—I lost consciousness. I knew nothing of what was going on around me. The pain brought me back to consciousness, however, as I hung upside down in my straps. I couldn't see anything either: I simply heard the drone of the constant attacks of the Messerschmitts whose bursts every now and again hit my plane. I didn't have the strength to undo the straps that were painfully cutting into my body. So I hung there helplessly for a long time waiting for help. I didn't care about anything, not even about the gunfire that occasionally hit my plane. I seemed to hang there for ages. After each pass I was amazed that I wasn't hit. Finally I could hear the planes flying off. Shortly thereafter some people from the nearby village ran over and freed me from my straps. I couldn't believe that I was still alive. . . ."

Then he stopped for a moment, breathing with difficulty.

"Those bastards!" he suddenly exploded. "They even fired on a beaten opponent, even on someone wounded! They ought to receive the same treatment," he finished.

He looked at me.

"There you have a powerful example. Two cases of humanitarianism: yours—the Polish—and theirs!"

"I hope you aren't angry with me talking you into this fatal flight?" I asked.

"You're crazy!" he exclaimed. "This could have happened to any of us; it's just too bad that it happened to me. Besides, I'm a little to blame myself: I should have watched my own tail better. Let that be a warning to you."

Our conversation was interrupted by the arrival of the doctor who notified Tadeusz that everything was ready to take Mirek to the hospital. We all hugged him symbolically, each delicately touching his shoulder and wishing him a speedy return to health. Since he didn't like mushy good-byes, we concluded our farewell by joking with him.

We stood for a long time waving good-bye to the departing ambulance that carried our beloved, gifted commander and irreplaceable friend away. We all believed he would return to us soon.

"And now the only one we don't know about is Karol," I said.

Everyone agreed. Since he hadn't returned by now, something must have happened to him. After all, was it possible that with the enemy's overwhelming numerical and technical superiority that we could get away without losses? Could we expect to get away scot-free, shooting down four enemy planes with only one wounded? Everything seemed to indicate that Karol's return was unlikely. Evidently—we reasoned—his death was the price we had to pay for our victories.

In the depths of my heart I felt an unbearable, overwhelming guilt. I had lost two friends to combat, and I felt responsible because I had goaded them into it. My colleagues tried to cheer me up by saying that, if not today, then perhaps tomorrow Karol would drop out of the sky unexpectedly, just as Edek did.

"Quickly to your planes for a briefing!" yelled Jaugsch. "We're moving to a new airfield."

"Dammit, what's going on?!" I looked with amazement at Władek. "We've already moved three times, why can't we stay put somewhere?"

There was a commotion around the planes as the mechanics removed the tree branches that camouflaged them. The group commander gave the orders to the squadron commanders.

Marian's plane was carried off to a safe distance in the field and set on fire. Unfit to fly, it had to be destroyed before the Germans arrived.

The group commander addressed those pilots who were to fly to the new airfield.

"In fifteen minutes we'll take off! We'll fly as a group to the airfield near the town of Osięciny. I'll take off first with the 141st Squadron, and after us Lieutenant Wilczewski with the 142nd. To your planes!"

We landed at dusk on a pleasant patch of land near the forest in Osięciny. It was very close to the small town and so in no time a considerable crowd of people showed up to help us roll our planes into the forest and camouflage them.

We found quarters in the residence of the Sanguszko Foundation where we were warmly greeted by its administrator and his wife, who put their entire house at our disposal. Our gracious guests immediately busied themselves with preparing something for us to eat. We had to rely on their generosity because our own mess-kitchen couldn't reach us till the following day.

Lieutenant Słonski, a pilot from our group who was presently attached to the air force staff unit, burst in on us like a bomb during the meal. He told us that Britain and France had declared war on Germany. This news didn't cause much of a stir among us, though. We treated it as nothing extraordinary, not connecting any special promise with it. Our situation was so perilous that only an immediate, powerful attack on the Western Front would force the Germans to transfer their forces and thus relieve the Polish front, which was breaking under the crushing superiority of the German armies. Unfortunately, as the coming days would show, nothing would betoken such a swift powerful action in the West. For the Germans, therefore, the threat of a war on two fronts didn't really exist. They could confidently concentrate their forces on Poland.

In attacking Poland Hitler threw all his forces to the east, virtually ignoring the danger to his western border. Evidently he felt sufficiently secure. Only subsequent analysis of the disposition of forces would show that an attack by the combined Anglo-French forces would have had a good chance of success and would have left Hitler in a very difficult situation. In the meantime leaflets were dropped on Germany, instead of bombs.

Słon—which is how we called Lieutenant Słonski—began to question Pisarek about the course of the recent battle. In the dim light of the oil lamp, his chubby face changed its expression under the influence of Marian's colorful description.

"Listen, Marian, who shot down the Junkers-87 over Inowrocław? I saw the fight because I was in the area. Then I saw three Messerschmitts jumped the Jedenastka and they went into a dive. It seemed as if he didn't have the least chance of coming out alive . . . do you think this might have been Pniak?"

Marian smiled the whole time, but let him finish. Nor did I interrupt his speculation, although I was itching to ask him what happened to the

German who bailed out. Marian told the amazed Słonski that the supposed fellow was sitting right next to him at the table. At first he didn't believe him, but he was finally convinced:

"So Pniak must still be alive!" he concluded.

"Tomorrow will tell!" interjected Władek Różycki optimistically. "Dammit."

The church bell rang the late hour as everyone, exhausted with the events of the day, began to look for a place to spend the night. I had already dropped off, sinking into a soft feather bed. And still from the next room I could hear the distinct sound of coins rattling and the characteristic rustle of cards shuffled by experienced hands.

CHAPTER EIGHT

Karol and the Reconnaissance Flight

THE EDGE OF THE FOREST PULSATED WITH LIFE. IN THE SHADE OF THE trees, the planes sat stripped, with their uncovered engines receiving necessary attention. Armorers sat in the cockpits examining the guns and repairing any defects. At the chief mechanic's insistence, the group commander had temporarily suspended action to give the ground crews time to give the planes and engines a thorough going over. They weren't exactly brand new and required exceptionally delicate care and maintenance. So we limited action to reconnaissance by one plane for the whole day.

At ten o'clock I returned from a reconnaissance mission without encountering any enemy planes. My only diversion was a game of "cat and mouse" with German antiaircraft that none too hospitably reminded me of their existence in the most unexpected and, it seems, most innocuous places. The entire area occupied by the Germans was dotted with antiaircraft positions, whose main task it was to protect troop movements against the probing eyes of our reconnaissance planes. They had no fear of us, however.

After I made my report, Wacek let me know that I was free till the evening.

"Did you have a chance to find a place to stay?" I asked him. "No," he replied. "They've already been assigned to others, and besides Wruś wants to take a look at your plane. When else can he do it?"

"Ready?!" Paweł suddenly yelled to me as he walked out of the nearby bushes.

"For what?" I asked.

"I've been waiting over an hour for you. Wacek gave me the car. We have to go into town to pick up some things: razor blades, aftershave. Come on, time's a wastin'."

When we were safely on our way he explained his true motives.

"You're really strange," Paweł chuckled. "Don't you know what's going on? I know a couple of hot babes in town. We rarely get a chance like this."

"Tell you what," I replied. "I really don't feel like it. I'd rather . . ."

"Rather what?" he interjected.

"I'd rather take a long bath when we get there."

"That's great. What a waste. You haven't even seen them and all you can think about is taking a bath. How can you do that?"

"It's war, dammit!" I fired back without thinking. "You have to realize that a guy can go weeks without seeing hot water."

Paweł thought I was joking until he noticed that I had put soap and towels in my bag. Still he couldn't believe it. When we arrived in town—and after I had explained myself to the girls—he simply refused to allow me to go my own way. He wouldn't give in. He felt compromised in front of his friends. Men are often strange.

Of course, during dinner Paweł told his friends about the circumstances accompanying my bath, giving free rein to his fertile imagination, so much so that his story became completely unsuitable for repetition.

Refreshed by my bath and feeling like a newborn baby, I went with Janek to hunt partridges which, from all accounts, were plentiful in the area. Although I had never gone hunting before, we somehow managed to bring something back.

Our prizes were accepted by our colleagues very cordially. Paweł cheered us with the news that while we were out enjoying ourselves hunting Tadeusz was also hunting and bagged a Henschel-126. We all then went to supper happy.

The dining room was bathed in semi-darkness. In its middle burned a small lamp that threw a discreet light on the long table at which a lively discussion was being carried on. When I came in, everyone went quiet though, which seemed a little strange to me. Their faces were sad, and they turned their eyes away from me. Taking an empty seat at the table, I had an uneasy feeling when I asked:

"Any news about Karol?"

"It's certain, he's a goner!" mumbled Władek Różycki in a somber voice.

I looked at him in disbelief.

"After all, yesterday you said the complete opposite. Have you changed your mind already?"

"You have to accept it. He's been away too long."

I poked around on the plate with my fork aimlessly, weighing the pros and cons in my mind as my colleagues distracted me with curious smiles directed to the seat next to me.

"Hey, what's going on?" I asked.

At that moment I heard a resounding laugh that could have only come from one person—Karol. I didn't even have time to get out of my chair before he seized me in his powerful grasp. It was only then that I understood the cryptic silence and curious looks. Karol was sitting behind the oven the entire time, listening to his own funeral. All of them—Karol included—had decided to play a trick on me.

When I had recomposed myself, I asked Karol some questions and had to wait a long time for the answers. But, finally, he kindly agreed to give me an answer. He told me he had shot down one Junkers-87, and damaged a second.

"I had pursued him too far and wasn't able to get back to you. Besides I wandered around a little bit!" he answered. "Returning from my pursuit I found out that I was running out of fuel. So I pulled my plane up in order to get a clear picture of my location. I could see the Vistula below me but the terrain was strange. My map indicated that I was somewhere in the vicinity of Włocławek. I had to make a decision. I had to land while there was still some fuel in my tank. I came down on a patch of ground alongside the road running toward Włocławek, believing that it would be easy for me to find some help there. Shortly thereafter Captain Stelmach came along . . ."

"And what was he doing there?" I interrupted. "He's supposed to be attached to Stachoń's operational staff."

"But the army headquarters is now in Włocławek, and the formation that we attacked had just returned from bombing the town. Apparently the Germans had bombed our headquarters, but fortunately they didn't do a good job. Their intelligence is very good and they act rapidly—I have to admit that, though. They know about all our movements immediately."

After supper, during which Karol told us all about the course of his two encounters, we sat down to cards and played into the night. Then we went to bed.

I was awakened from my sleep, however, by someone grabbing at me abruptly. At first I couldn't understand what Tadeusz, who kept shaking me, wanted.

"Get up, get up! It's very important! Get up right away!"

I shook the cobwebs out and sat up in the bed.

"What's happening?!" I exclaimed apprehensively.

"Nothing, quiet! Get up right away, you're going on a very important mission."

"Now, at night? When will I be able to get some sleep?!" I growled as I got dressed.

Tadeusz told me that he had been up that night too. He had just gotten back from headquarters.

"Whom do you want as your wingman?" he asked. "Go wake him up." Without hesitation I replied:

"Śmiegielski."

Tadeusz told me to report to him when I was ready. While I finished getting dressed, I tried to figure out what might be the reason for dragging me out of bed. I drew the shutters to blacken out the windows. Outside it was still very foggy. A moment later I reported to the group commander, ready for action.

"I'll drive you immediately to the airfield. You'll take off while it's still dark. But when you get to the reconnaissance area it'll be light. The commander of the army has to have information as soon as possible about a German crossing of the Vistula. The crossing is expected at different points, and your mission is to find these points."

Tracing with a pencil on the map, he indicated our route as well as the section of the Vistula we had to reconnoiter in depth: where the enemy was preparing a crossing or where a crossing was already underway.

"This information is very important and urgent," Tadeusz continued, "so return immediately to base as fast as you can, without getting into any fights. Remember that a lot depends on time! Try to observe as much as you can: the direction in which units are moving, the length of enemy columns, etc. That's it. Let's go! Śmiegielski, I'm sure, is waiting at the car."

I explained our mission to Corporal Śmiegielski as we rode to the airfield.

"Keep your eyes open," I told him, "because if something happens to me you'll have to complete the mission."

Śmiegielski was a good, intelligent pilot and liked his work. That's why I chose him. I trusted him completely and although I often called him a "turkey egg" because of the freckles with which nature had adorned his face, we were good friends.

We took off together from the unlighted airfield in the dead of night. Our running lights were the only thing that flashed in the darkness, and a moment later we were climbing, heading in a northeasterly direction. An impenetrable fog surrounded us, and the monotonous drone of the engine worked like a narcotic on me. About a half an hour later, the silhouettes of our planes became visible against the background of the gray sky. Approaching the vicinity of Solec, in an area occupied by the enemy, we turned off our lights, as in the east the grayness of the sky began to give way to a grimy blue.

In the area from Toruń to Solec and the bridge at Fordoń, I didn't see any traces of enemy crossings of the Vistula. Ignoring Bydgoszcz, we turned in the direction of Koronowo. I closely watched the river as well as the highways and field roads. Before Świecie, from an altitude of 800 meters, I saw, in the distance, a suspicious dark band across the Vistula. Since there was no bridge connecting Świecie and Chełmno, I guessed that this must be the crossing we were looking for. I waved my hand to indicate the direction to Śmiegielski. He nodded his head to show me that he saw it too, then I turned slowly to the left, diving deep into enemy territory.

Now I could see much more clearly. There was no doubt about it, the Germans had built a pontoon bridge between Świecie and Chełmno. Now we had to find out what kind of forces, and in what strength, were taking part in the crossing. We took off for Świecie. Against the blue background of the sky I could see the first puffs of antiaircraft artillery exploding around us. I pushed the throttle forward to full speed and dove in the direction of the crossing. Śmiegielski made an S-turn and hung on my tail.

"He's crazy!" I thought to myself as I watched his maneuver.

Large concentrations of men and matériel were pouring into the mouth of the crossing, and antiaircraft artillery started to crackle as it tried to create a barrier against our attack. Black plumes of flak exploded all around us. Things started to get hot. I choked the plane more, standing it on its nose to descend from altitude to attack. The enemy vehicles that saw us stopped unexpectedly, and masses of people jumped out of them in a panic, running in different directions looking for protection in the ditches along the road.

We went on the attack, raining fire down on the confused mass who hugged the ground like a swarm of locusts in their dirty gray uniforms covering every patch of green. Along our flight path, directly at the end of the bridge-head, was a cannon belching fire from its rapid-fire barrel. My gun sight moved rapidly over the most convenient targets: tanks, armored-cars . . . I clenched my teeth in disgust at the carnage I was caus-ing. The enemy soldiers then suddenly jumped up as if shocked, waving their arms in the air. For the moment I stopped firing and turned my plane toward the artillery position on the riverbank. After a brief clash the cannon stopped firing. I then attacked the pontoon bridge, never letting up on my fire. Across the bridge there were tanks and armored cars moving about, firing at us with their machine guns. In an instant the river beside the bridge teemed with the heads of Germans who had jumped into the water to save themselves. A couple of the cars that were hit "showed their true colors and ran," and those that weren't able to take cover littered the bridge with their remains. I released the trigger only when I had got to Chełmno; the first German tanks had already reached there.

The crossing was only in its initial stage. Now beyond the reach of the German antiaircraft fire I pulled my plane up, looking back for Śmiegielski. He was attacking the pontoon bridge too. "I hope he doesn't get hit," I thought to myself, seeing how dangerous the situation was. His plane flew amid a halo of gunfire and black puffs of smoke from flak bursts.

He was halfway across the bridge. Just a second more and . . . I breathed a sigh of relief: He had made it. He pulled alongside of me and shaking his head in his hand gave me to understand the ordeal we had been through. Then we hot-footed it home as quickly as possible to deliver the news. After landing I reported the course of the mission immediately.

"Why did you attack?" Tadeusz asked angrily. "After all, I had expressly told you the significance of this mission. What would have happened if you had been shot down?"

"There still would have been Śmiegielski," I replied.

"And if he were hit? From your report it follows that you had come up against a large group. Things could have turned out badly . . . ," he said.

"I had to reconnoiter in detail in what force the enemy was crossing! That meant that I had to get a close look, and in that situation . . . ," I answered.

Tadeusz didn't say anything after that. He just shook his head incredulously.

A moment later an RWD-8 took off with the report to army headquarters.

"Hey Śmiegielski, let's go get some breakfast," I called to him.

On the way, we discussed our joint mission.

"I didn't think that it would go so smoothly for us," Śmiegielski said. "Flying behind you, I was sure you were going to be shot down."

"And I was afraid that you would never get through the enemy barrage . . . ," I replied.

Śmiegielski heaved a sigh of relief.

"Despite everything a strong attack isn't fatal," he said. "We weren't even scratched . . . Sure, I sweated as if I was in childbirth and had cold feet enough for two hundred. But I squeezed all the juice I could out of my plane, and I came out in one piece."

By the time we had returned to the airfield the "Erwudziak"[1] already landed, bringing new orders for the group, and the commander called a briefing for the pilots.

---

[1] Translator's note: *Erwudziak* refers to the two-seat RWD-8 trainer monoplane that squadrons used for liaison.

CHAPTER NINE

The Defense of the Bridges at Toruń

WE HAD RECEIVED ORDERS TO DEFEND THE BRIDGES AT TORUŃ AGAINST an imminent air attack. An enemy action was expected in connection with the shift of large units of our army across the Vistula. Since the place had only one vehicular bridge, it became very important to hold it for our troops for at least a whole day. The order expressly mentioned the defense of vehicular as well as train bridges at all cost.

Defensive patrols were to overlap so there would be no gaps the Germans could exploit. This meant the 141st Squadron would take off first, and the 142nd an hour later.

Half an hour later six Jedenastkas took off for Toruń under Tadeusz's command.

There were several overlapping patrols during the morning, none of which met enemy planes. In the meantime, however, the Germans had unleashed an attack in the south. Marian was flying with both flights of his squadron over the bridge when, from the north, fourteen Junkers-87s packed with bombs, and without fighter escort, approached. They followed along the Vistula, only minutes away from their target. As they approached the bridge, they armed their bombs. The calm voice of what was surely their commander could be heard over the radio giving final orders before the attack.

Suddenly there was commotion over the airwaves. "They've spotted us!" Quickly, nervous warnings were issued: "*Achtung, Achtung! Polnischer Jägerverband!*" ["Attention, attention! Polish fighters."] "'Osy' ["Wasps"] patrolling over the bridge."

According to the testimony of captured airmen, the Germans called us "wasps" in this sector of the front, which was an ironic turn of events since our code name for ourselves was "bees" ["*pszczoły*"]. Apparently "pszczoły" was difficult for them to pronounce, so they called us "osy" ["wasps"]. I can't say if it flattered us at the time.

Thus the "osy" ["wasps"] buzzed around violently, and led by Marian, furiously attacked the Germans head-on, scattering their formation before they had time to reach their target. In the first attack one of the Junkers was hit by Marian and fell in flames. The scattered Germans began to dump their bombs anywhere they could so as to lighten their planes, gain speed, and try to distance themselves from our planes in a furious dive to ground level. One of our Jedenastkas was hit and trailed a dark ribbon of smoke. It jettisoned its fiery fuel tank. Ensign Drybański, with a wounded arm and slightly burned, landed engineless on a sandbar in the Vistula. The rest of the planes, breaking off their pursuit of the Germans, returned to defend the bridges. The German attack had been scattered and neutralized. The army columns still calmly crossed over the bridge, hurrying in the anticipated direction of concentration.

When we replaced Marian's patrol over the bridge, we could see five Jedenastkas flying about below us. The sixth rested on the sandbar on the riverbank.

Our patrol passed without any surprises. Nor did the Germans carry out any actions against the bridges later in the day. The sun dipped slowly in the west when the group commander showed up to replace us.

After landing I told the mechanics to fill up the plane and put my parachute in the car. Then I went over to the radio station, which maintained constant contact with the remaining patrol in the air.

"Well Stasiu!" Marian called, "how many did you get?"

"Give me a break," I replied angrily. "We hung over those bridges like balloons on a string, and there was no sign of Germans. You frightened them all away."

"So much the better," interrupted Paweł. "If they really wanted to, they could have smashed us as well as the bridge . . . for what could we six have done if a large gang of them descended on us?"

We began to consider the possible German plans when, in the course of our discussion, the radio officer jumped out of his car and in an excited voice shouted:

"Gentlemen! the Queen Bee [which was the group commander's code name] requests immediate assistance. He has encountered large German formations!"

Not waiting for orders, Paweł, Wieprzkowicz, and I instantly ran to our planes. Without even donning my suit, I started my engine and was in the air a moment later, flying at full speed in the direction of Toruń. The three of us spread out as we climbed. In the air I put on my flying cap and buckled my straps which, for some reason, were slightly loose. I took aim with my gun sight, but something wasn't right here either: It was too low. Sitting comfortably in my seat I felt something missing. I finally realized what it was, but just to be sure I reached around to my back. No doubt about it, in my haste I had completely forgotten about my parachute. A shiver went up my back, but I decided to go on. So I pushed the throttle forward to catch up with Paweł and Wieprzkowicz.

Before us stood Toruń.

Poking about in the clouds, I still couldn't see anything. As the town came nearer, at an altitude of 200 meters, I could see three Messerschmitts circling over the bridge. They were far apart. As we closed in on the bridges, the Germans made a wide turn and flew off in a westerly direction. The bridge was still intact. I couldn't see enemy or friendly planes in the area except for the three Messerschmitts that didn't attack. Instead, we followed them up to a higher altitude. Sparkling in the dazzling rays of the setting sun, their sleek silhouettes evoked admiration and a burning envy. They circled higher and higher, never letting us get close.

"Paweł, you go north," I shouted into the microphone. "Wieprzkowicz, east, and I'll try to cut them off from the west. We'll meet in the middle!"

The Germans burst out laughing when they overheard my message, which surprised me because I thought that they should have been the ones to make an attack. What chance would we have had? And yet, against all logic, we were the ones to join the fight, the ones who took the initiative. In this hopeless pursuit, in which we were never able to close the ring, and the enemy remained constantly above us, my altimeter already read 4,000 meters. We had already flown far past Toruń, with the Germans continuing to retreat to the west, drawing us along with them. When the sun went down they dove for the ground and we lost sight of them against the dark background. There was nothing else to do but follow from where we had last seen them.

It became urgent now, however, for us to return. I felt angry with the encounter. I couldn't get the sleek, modern silhouettes of the enemy fighters out of my mind.

In the history of air combat in both world wars, there has perhaps never been a more incongruous juxtaposition than that of the Jedenastka and the Messerschmidt-BF109.

I had hardly gotten out of my plane when Tadeusz came down on me for flying without a parachute.

"I was in a hurry. I forgot," I told him, "and it was too late to turn back. After all, you requested immediate assistance."

Disarmed by my explanation, he only looked at me with pity.

"And if you had to bail out, what then?"

"Yeah, I thought about that too."

"And what did you come up with?"

"I got the creeps!" I answered calmly.

"If they had shot you down somewhere without a parachute," Paweł interjected, "all that would be left of you would be your boots."

"Or not," I replied. "I'll always try to make sure that these boots have an owner."

This day belonged to the 141st Squadron, which registered two victories without any fatalities, having only one wounded—Ensign Drybański. Drybański was taken to the hospital in Toruń. His plane was unrecoverable since there was no time or possibility to move it to a safe place.

In the meantime the group commander ordered another move. All planes had to be ready to fly early next morning.

During the night the rest of our army crossed the rescued bridge, undisturbed by the enemy, and took up new positions.

After a week of fighting we now had to take leave of our army, which was then left alone, deprived of air support and cooperation. We were ordered to join with the Warsaw pursuit brigade, which then created a force consisting of two groups and the Krakowski squadron. The new base was on the Vistula southeast of Kazimierz, in the area of Bełżec. This meant a significant jump—from Pomerania to central Poland. For the aircrews this wasn't a big deal. Nor did the distance make much of a difference. But the transfer was another matter for the ground crews, who faced dangerous and unforeseeable difficulties. They were exposed to constant air attacks along the entire route. In addition, as a result of gaps that existed in many sections of our defensive lines, there was the danger of being surrounded by enemy detachments and captured.

The order to leave our army, with which we had operated since the beginning of hostilities, gave us doubts. We began to think about the causes of the decision and came up with different ideas. The most probable was the notion that by concentrating our fighter forces we would be able to defend the central part of the country in the most effective way, rather than to disperse our forces into individual groups operating with particular armies at the fronts. The concentration of forces in one sector might produce the best results.

Tadeusz told us that this wasn't the only or even the most important reason. The change in the conception of operation resulted—he thought—from a lack of matériel, which doubtless was beginning to affect all fighting units. Our capacity to operate decreased with every day, and seriously threatened to eliminate our ability to fight as such due to the losses that we had suffered not only in combat with the enemy but also because of difficult conditions, a lack of suitable airfields, and the inability to guarantee maintenance of our engines and planes. The use of old and worn-out equipment threatened catastrophe, and in the meantime not one plane had been replaced. Long-term action was impossible without new planes, despite an ample supply of pilots. Under these conditions a concentration of forces provided the only answer. It permitted us to carry out at least minimal combat action—we thought—on the most important sectors with the maximum economy of irreplaceable planes. Nevertheless, we didn't know the real circumstances of the commander's decision. We also lacked much of the information needed to form an opinion about the situation in general.

As a result of our departure a panic seized our ground crews. Late into the night they beset us with questions about what to do. The next morning, however, I could see that they had packed their bags.

On the 6th of September the general order was given to retreat behind the Vistula. The picture of the Polish defensive situation became increasingly clear and . . . tragic. The German attacks had broken through the Polish front in many sectors. The battle of Piotrków ended with the defeat of the Pomorze army under the command of General Dąb-Biernacki. The road to Warsaw was open. The German army pushed through Rawa Mazowiecka in the direction of the capital, at the same time Łódź was within reach of enemy action. On the southern front Polish units were forced to retreat to the Danube line, and in the north the enemy crossed the Narew and was moving on Modlin. Thus the Narew had already ceased to be a line of defense that Polish forces could use to defend against attacks from the north—using the Vistula and the Danube in the south for support. The sinister German ring grew ever tighter.

The air was calm. A slight breeze drifted about our planes as we flew in combat formation on a southeasterly course across the Vistula toward Kazimierz. The horizon became increasingly obscure. Near Warsaw the sky grew gray and dirty along one side of our route. As far as the eye could see, there was evidence of fighting. The entire horizon was enveloped in the smoke of burning cities, towns, and villages, which constituted "important military targets" for the Nazi Luftwaffe. Under my wings passed the smoldering ruins of poor, rural cottages, the ruins of country farms. Brute force had brought death to our people, and ruin to the countryside.

A villainy was perpetrated to which the entire world remained an indifferent spectator.

I could smell the stench of burning in my nostrils. I became bitter and felt a painful weight in my heart. Our impotence was mortifying.

I was seized by successive feelings of pain, impotence, and despair. I learned to hate, and involuntarily pulled the trigger.

Out of this murky smoke emerged the narrow, silvery ribbon of the Vistula. To make things worse, its riverbed had contracted and its gently rolling waters illuminated its shoals. The summer wore on in its heat and humidity. Even nature was against us. The river, which should have played the role of a natural line of defense, was transformed into a shallow stream useless as a significant barrier.

Below us on the right lay the picturesque town of Kazimierz. A few minutes later we landed on the hard, bumpy field of the estate at Bełżec. The planes were concealed in the thick, wooded undergrowth. On the brigade commander's order, the mechanics of the 3rd Warsaw group and Krakowski squadron, servicing us until our own ground crews arrived, immediately began to paint out the squadron insignia on our planes. This was a source of discord for us, because we didn't think that such an extreme measure was necessary. Each squadron had its own tradition, its own spirit. We were very attached to our insignia, even more so because we had already achieved a number of victories under it. Nonetheless, our beloved ducks with their spread wings—blue for the 141st Squadron, green for the 142nd—soon disappeared. The visible sign of what tied us together into a cohesive unit disappeared. It would be difficult now to recognize our own planes. There ceased to be anything to distinguish them from one another. Instead, now they had become something gray and dull.

I also lost my original plane, number "66," so I decided to give this plane the name "Zosia." I painted it myself in white on the fuselage to make it easier for me to find my plane among the others. The christening, unfortunately, had to take place without the attendance of a patroness or the traditional bottle of champagne. But I did receive a number of taunts from my colleagues who thought that my action demonstrated a stubborn persistence of sentimentality.

Around the command post, which was situated in an open area under a large tent, I met some colleagues from training school: Tolek Łokuciewski, Mirek Ferić, and Janek Daszewski, who everyone called "Pan Antoń," whom I hadn't seen since leaving training school in Dęblin.

"Hey, Stasiu!" Tolek greeted me. "You still alive? I see that the Germans haven't gotten their hands on you yet . . ."

"It's still a little too early for that," I replied, greeting my old colleague. "Meanwhile I see you've been lucky . . . where's Zumbach hiding?"

"He's been in the hospital for a month. He crashed and broke his leg; he's recuperating now. We were landing in formation, and our squadron commander was so close to him that Janek crashed into a passing ambulance. Of course, he rolled over and there were only little bits left of his plane and the ambulance. I'd like to know how he'll get out of Warsaw because the Germans are pushing forward like pigs to the trough. I hope they don't slam the door shut on him. . . ."

"And what's wrong with Pan Antoń that you're so dejected?" I asked as I turned to Janek Daszewski.

He really looked the very picture of misery. He simply made a face at me and waved his hand. Tolek, however, told me that since eating some fruit he had been suffering from dysentery.

"He really likes to be left alone now, and doesn't want any company!" he concluded caustically.

Pan Antoń overheard his friend's words with an indulgent smile.

The pursuit brigade to which we were now assigned had operated during the first days of the war in the defense of Warsaw from an airfield near Zielonka. Its pilots had fought their first battles over Warsaw and its vicinity with mixed success. Tolek described their exploits with humor:

"It was a mixed bag. We encountered some of "them" on the outskirts of Warsaw, but they gave us a hard time. Some of our people were killed, some wounded. 'Ox' (Mirosław Ferić) bailed out. He was lucky he could because the Germans shot off his joystick!"

My protracted, astonished "ooo!" brought Ox out from hiding:

"I was so exhausted that holding the shot-off joystick in my hand I didn't initially realize what had happened. And my plane was already in a tailspin. What was I to do? I didn't raise a finger! I couldn't bail out, but this was probably better because the sky was full of Germans. If I had bailed out right away they would have gone after me just like they did with Feliks Szyszka. . . ."

"What about Feliks, is he alive?" I asked.

"He's in the hospital seriously wounded; perhaps he's pulled through . . . his plane caught fire during a fight, and so he naturally bailed out. Then they went after him! The Messerschmitts fired at him all the way to the ground, even though he was wounded and burned." He sighed. "I don't know what will happen with him. He was shot up pretty bad, and had many broken bones. . . ."

We talked a bit more about the commanders who were standing nearby, and I recognized our commander from training school—Sznuka—among them. He was talking with Pamuła, the first commander of the pursuit brigade, who had an unpleasant experience with two Messerschmitts and—as Tolek said—"had to bail out" with his hands burned. Tolek openly praised his group commander Captain Krasnodębski. The Germans tried to shoot at him too, but despite being burned, he refused to go to the hospital. Although he could no longer fly, he was given command of the group.

"They pretty well cleaned you out," I said.

"Inasmuch as . . . we didn't do too bad as far as pilots are concerned, but worse regarding planes. Our 'expenditure' in them was much greater."

Tadeusz interrupted our chat, announcing our new assignment. So we had to break up. I could already hear Tolek calling from a distance:

"Just watch your step! We need a fourth tonight. . . ."

I thought to myself that I was going to have to make an appearance. There was no mention of poker, but we understood each other perfectly well, and I had no doubts that he was not talking about a fourth for bridge.

During patrol we didn't encounter any enemy planes and had to "satisfy" ourselves with the view of Warsaw burning and the bombed out, enormous molehill of an airfield at Dęblin, as well as the picture of the remains of Garwolin, which now existed only on the map. The little town had gone up in smoke.

The day passed without any unusual events; however a certain uneasiness was felt which passed only in the evening. There was no end of talk about combat, which soon changed into discussions of air-combat tactics in general. New fighter tactics—new ways of fighting, which we would use in later battles over other skies, were born on that unknown airfield at Bełżec. We were the first cadre of fighter pilots upon whose shoulders fell the full weight of the modern German air force. We were the first to gain experience—paid for in blood. We were also the first to draw conclusions from this experience. Sad conclusions. The disregard of air force development before the war and incompetence of command during it were the main causes of our inability to offer an effective resistance to the Luftwaffe.

Lieutenant Januszkiewicz described his fight over Warsaw with a Messerschmitt-110 piloted by a German major who was a veteran of the Spanish Civil War. The German, an experienced fighter pilot and member of the famous "Condor Legion," resolved to decide his duel with Januszkiewicz at any cost. Although he had lost his rear gunner and Januszkiewicz had damaged one of his engines, he continued to fight on, even though the slower, but more agile Jedenastka tenaciously hung on his tail. Finally after having received a direct hit and being wounded, he made a forced landing in a field near our airfield. Januszkiewicz refused to fire on his defeated victim, but circled above until the German had climbed out of his plane, and watched him so that he wouldn't escape. The major was taken by ambulance to the airfield where he insisted on meeting his victor. His astonishment was all the greater when he met the small, fair-haired lieutenant who courteously bowed to him and expressed his regrets at his suffering. This was the third German that Januszkiewicz had shot down over Warsaw and captured.

CHAPTER TEN

Patrol

THE FOREST HAD COME TO LIFE. ALL AROUND THERE WAS THE BUZZ OF human voices and the roar of engines warming up. Thick clouds of dust rose from the bushes. Suddenly three planes of the Krakowski squadron popped out of the bushes of the neighboring airfield across the road. Their engines roared and a moment later their silhouettes rose above us, flying north. A moment later the growl of two flights from the pursuit brigade crossed the airfield, trailing clouds of smoke.

Things were quiet for us, however. It looked like we were going to remain grounded due to the absence of our ground crew. And our group commander, who was called to a briefing with the regimental commander, did not return for a suspiciously long time.

We weren't happy with our new assignment. Everything happened here—we thought—lethargically, haphazardly, and too cautiously. The commanders lacked the spark, the gumption to inspire their subordinates. Everyone sensed this listless attitude, which frustrated any kind of genuine initiative.

"Our Napoleon's back," said Zieliński, who often called Tadeusz "Napoleon" because of his size. "But he must be angry because his head is drooping!"

Tadek was really quite irritated but he didn't say much, and he only waved his hand in answer to our insistent entreaties and ordered Wacek to put together a patrol.

I quickly ran up to the commander because Paweł winked at me and pointed to himself to indicate to me that he had already been chosen.

"Wacek, you got a place for me?" I asked.

"Yes, yes!" he rebuffed me. "I would like to go too. It's impossible to please everyone."

"Oh great!" Paweł shouted. "The commander's gonna direct us from the ground!"

"Quiet!" he retorted. "Zenker, Skalski, and Pniak report to Tadziu!"

"And what about me, am I going?" asked Zieliński, his feelings hurt. Karol rubbed his hands together in glee.

"Well, you see, if it weren't for me!" Paweł nudged me with his elbow. After a short briefing we set off for our planes.

"Let's take off together over those trees!" Paweł decided as we went, pointing to the trees at the edge of the airfield. "Don't worry, you won't crash into them, Stasiu, as long as your engine doesn't conk out!"

"Don't jinx me! You'd be laughing out of the other side of your mouth if it happened to you!"

"I'm not worried," he joked.

With difficulty we finally located our planes, and a moment later I was taxiing over toward Paweł and Karol who were already in position. Paweł raised his hand giving the "ready" signal. I nodded and at the last moment pointed at the spreading trees in the path of our takeoff and broke into a broad grin as he pointed at me.

The planes gathered speed over the hard field. Paweł managed to turn to me and flash a taunting smile. I had to cut the throttle not to overtake him. Then I could see him begin to look about nervously in his cockpit. His propeller began to slow down and his engine stopped turning. The trees came closer, closer, but it was too late to put on the brakes. I pushed my throttle all the way forward and, jumping slightly aside, I pulled my plane up over the barrier. Karol did the same and we ascended together, but . . . with a gap between us. "He crashed after all," I thought to myself as I watched Paweł from the air. Not being able to apply the brakes and with a dead engine, he was still able to pass safely through the trees, cross the road, and come down on the ploughed field. He rolled on for a few more meters, and for a brief moment rose up after which, as if in anger, he bumped his tail smack against the ground—and there was Paweł lying on his back. Of course, this picture raised our spirits as I climbed with

Karol in the direction of Lublin, leading the patrol in Paweł's place over the forests around Lublin, which contained concentrations of our forces that were being harassed by German air attacks.

After a half hour of patroling, we noticed a couple of dark specks on the misty horizon flying parallel to us, a little bit ahead. I signaled Karol as I headed in their direction to try to cut them off. The specks became increasing larger. The entire time Karol remained behind me because his plane was slower. "It wasn't for nothing that Wruś worked on my plane," I thought to myself as I noticed the difference. "He did such a good job, it's straining so much that it's shaking. If only he hadn't worked on the engine!"

A few minutes later I had intercepted the formation of bombers and their silhouettes became clear. They were Junkers-86s. This was the first time I had encountered this type of plane, which was significantly slower than the Dorniers, Heinkels, and Junkers-87s. There were nine of them flying in flights of three without fighter escort.

I was slightly above them when I descended. The distance between us decreased slowly, but decidedly, as I came out right behind them. My finger inched toward the trigger and I raised my head a little. But I couldn't take my eye off the gun sight. There wasn't time. A few seconds more and . . . the gunners on the bombers caught me in a crossfire. Dark puffs of smoke cut across the blue sky. It was already too late to withdraw from the unanticipated and dangerous attack. I was in the middle, being fired at from the front and both sides, enveloped in an increasingly thick field of fire. As the distance between us grew shorter, their fire became increasingly dangerous, almost hitting me. Reflexively I crouched in my cockpit. A second more, a half-second . . . the leading plane shook in my gun sight. I didn't see anything else around.

I pulled the trigger. One, two, three bursts and the Junkers started to trail smoke.

He continued to fire at me, but dumped his entire bomb-load, which, obviously, had now become a liability to him. The fact that he was hit, though, didn't prevent him from maintaining his place in the formation, which continued on to its target. The fire I received became increasingly accurate, pelting my fuselage and wings ominously. So I dove out of their midst, attacking for the moment the planes on the right wing, whose return fire was not concentrated and therefore weak.

I attacked the plane in the middle from his rear right side. He too soon began to trail a ribbon of black smoke. I attacked again. But this time my guns went dead. I had run out of ammunition. So I pulled off, but stayed with the formation for a little while to see if either of the planes would fall out of formation and try to return to base. The feathered blades of the damaged engines gleamed in the sun, with smoke trailing behind. I looked around for Karol, hoping that he would be able to finish the attack on at least one of the planes. Unfortunately he was too far behind. What a difference a small discrepancy in speed made!

I swung around and returned to him. We circled for a little while in the area, hoping that the Germans would return by the same route. Finally our time was up and we had to return to base. During the return flight we flew close together and I could see Karol gesticulating, nodding his head, and smiling. But I couldn't understand why he was so amused.

In landing I felt a powerful thump. My plane swung around in an S, grudgingly and stiffly rolling along the field. The thumping of the wheels told me that both tires had been punctured. Seeing the mechanics running over toward me, I switched off the ignition at the end of the runway.

"They shot you up pretty good!" remarked the mechanics as they pushed the plane into the woods. "Tell me about it!"

I answered all their questions and then headed over toward a crowd of pilots where Karol was making his report to the group commander.

"Why he didn't break off, I'll never know!" he told the group. Then turning to me he asked, "Why did you fly into the middle of them? Don't you like living? I couldn't even make you out in the confusion around you. I tell you that this guy is so cool it's incredible. He went right into their middle. The Germans beat on him like a drum and . . . nothing, not even a scratch!"

Although Karol spoke in a sincere manner, everyone laughed. I wasn't able to convince him that my target had been the formation's leader and that I had to jump into the middle to reach him.

"Anyway, I didn't go that far into the middle, Karol. I stayed a little behind them . . .," I said.

"Don't try to explain!" he interrupted. "I saw how you attacked them! You should have gone after the wingman first, and then the formation's leader!"

I eventually admitted that he was right. I regretted not having attacked from the outside. Perhaps I would have gotten one of them. Instead—they all got away.

"I wish I had your luck!" sighed Karol. "You must have been born under a lucky star . . ."

"Well, well here comes our commander!" he said as he pointed at Paweł. "He's managed to brush himself off."

"Well, who do we have here?" I said, acknowledging Paweł. "Didn't you gauge the height of the trees? You're lucky that the person who planted them was thinking of you, otherwise you'd be on the way to the hospital right now!"

"Joking aside," he interrupted, "do you remember that something came over me before we took off? Only I didn't think that I would be the one to end up in the trees. This time you made it."

"My plane, Paweł, runs like a fine Swiss watch," I replied. "But it looks like you're going to have to go out and pick up the parts of your plane after it's been removed."

"The mechanics are already working on it," he said, "fixing the fuse-lage a little, changing the propeller. It'll fly again . . . anyway, your crate needs repairs too! So you'll be grounded with me, at least for today!" he said.

In the meantime out from among the farm buildings of the estate emerged a column of trucks that we could see included our group's ground crew. "Our little friends have finally arrived!" rejoiced Tadeusz. "At least we'll now have our own mechanics."

They poured out of the trucks grimy, covered with dust, tired, but happy that they had finally reached their destination. We were together again. You really have to know the air force to understand how deep the tie is that binds these two, seemingly different, groups together: pilots and their mechanics—especially in wartime. "We're together again"—this statement meant more to us than if it had been said between loving spouses.

It seems that the group's ground crew had been intercepted en route by German detachments advancing on Warsaw, which suddenly appeared at the head of their column. The courageous attitude of Master Sergeant Łyduch, who decided to fight, bore positive results. A fight began with an armed German motorcycle patrol. After suffering some losses, the patrol had to withdraw, opening the road to Warsaw. The group reached its goal without any losses in men or matériel, bringing with them, in addition, some "prizes" in the form of substantial numbers of weapons. These came from a store in one of the abandoned towns. The proprietor who fled before the Germans decided to save the weapons by giving them to the Polish army. Amateur hunters immediately picked out the best shotguns: the Belgian and the English ones.

After a brief rest for the group, Paweł left at the head of a column of cars for Dęblin to get fuel, which was now running low. We even had to limit our flying time to conserve a certain emergency supply in case we were forced, by rapidly advancing enemy forces, to make another sudden move. According to unconfirmed reports, Radom had already been over-run by the enemy. The distance was becoming too small to dismiss the possibility of a sudden appearance of German patrols in our area. The situation required that we maintain the utmost caution.

Since my plane had to be repaired after its last flight, and I was therefore grounded for the time being, Stach Zieliński and I went over to the neighboring group to hear what they were gossiping about. Along the way we agreed that our "Napoleon" certainly had a bone to pick with the regiment's commander, which only aggravated an already bad relationship. Right from the very beginning we felt in a certain sense second-class citizens. The colonel favored the units that were under his command before the war. Perhaps you couldn't blame him, but he should at least have tried to give the appearance of impartiality. At least he was able to avoid some provocative situations.

"I wish we were going back to Toruń," I sighed. "How long is this retreat going to last? I even hate to say the word: *retreat*."

"We even have to go out hunting for fuel, and the war's only eight days old," Stach replied. "I don't know what's gonna happen in the future. The road back to Toruń will be long and hard. The Germans won't give up so easily what they've already won. Our only hope is with France! If they don't start moving in the west, the Krauts'll push us into the Polesian marshes."

We got to the operational tent where we met Janusz Łabicki whom we hardly recognized, he was so wrapped up in bandages. Only his eyes peaked out from under the folds. A defective engine forced him to land on rough terrain. He smashed his plane and hit his head against the instrument panel.

"He looks like a mummy, except he's not a few thousand years old," explained Tolek. "And who do we have here, Stasiu and his twin?" he asked as he turned to me.

"Unfortunately . . . and you, did you have any luck?" I asked.

"Not much. Ox shot down a Henschel-126; outside of that I didn't see anything. For some reason the Germans aren't active in this area. There was action around Warsaw," he sighed. "We couldn't complain . . . there were plenty of planes, in fact too many. Maybe we'll return there. I hear that we'll have to . . ."

"It seems that's only wishful thinking. After all, the Germans are already somewhere in the area; why do we have to go looking for them?" someone said.

"They'll encircle us for sure if we stay here! Better to get ready to move in the opposite direction, east!" said another.

"Provided it's not too far!" said someone else.

All our opinions were based merely on suspicions. No accurate information about the general situation reached us. We felt as if we were in the Stone Age, not in the age of electricity and radio. Our means of communication were inadequate. We didn't even have an operational staff to create a dynamic picture of the course of the war.

Paweł returned in the evening with only a few cans of gas. Dęblin had already gone up in smoke. Its airfield now had only a guard and one officer, Major Wawrzyniak, who helped him in collecting small quantities of fuel. The entire training center had been moved to the southeast. The mobilization stores were left to the mercy of fate. Dęblin, which so recently had been vibrating with life, was dead. All that remained were smashed buildings, remnants of hangars, and a bombed-out airstrip.

The weather continued to be an ally of the invaders. Day after day passed with sunny, warm, blue skies unblemished with even the hint of a cloud: in other words, the best imaginable conditions to conduct air operations on a large scale. The winged spearhead of the invaders smashed our defenses with its attacks, opening the road to unending streams of motorized German columns. The dry, hardened ground easily bore the weight of the heavy enemy vehicles. Under these conditions, even the notoriously poor state of our roads ceased to be our ally. The enemy waded across our rivers, which scarcely retarded the momentum of his attack. Only heavy downpours and low cloud cover would have been able to impede this avalanche, to weaken its force on the ground and in the air. The Luftwaffe would then have been grounded at its bases and deprived of the conditions to carry out operations. For the present, however, the Germans continued to possess the initiative and carried out attacks under the most favorable conditions. They were constantly in the vicinity, constantly on our heels, appearing in the least expected places, even in our rear.

The news spread rapidly that the Warsaw group and the Krakowski squadron had received orders to change airfields and that the Germans had captured the bridge-head in Puławy, with its bridge across the Vistula intact.

Tadziu and I leaned over the map spread out on the ground.

"During your reconnaissance mission, fly north along the Vistula," he explained. "But keep to the right side, paying close attention to the bridge at Puławy. Find out who's holding it."

Pushing his finger in the direction of Dęblin almost to Warsaw, he traced the route of the mission.

Jaugsch was flying with me on his first combat mission. He poked about in the skies, searching for something. But both the sky and the ground were empty. Puławy and the bridge across the Vistula appeared before us. We descended from our assigned altitude, circling over the bridge a few times. Both sides of it were completely quiet. So I flew a little farther west. But even there I didn't see any evidence of the enemy's presence. I could see that the bridge, already abandoned by our forces, didn't seem to be in the enemy's hands. I climbed back up, flying back toward Dęblin. Against the background of the Vistula in the distance loomed the silhouette of a twin-engine plane. We gradually advanced on the Dornier-215, which flew at low altitude along the Vistula. He hadn't seen us yet because he was flying leisurely, reconnoitering the terrain. Suddenly I could see short, dark clouds of combustion shooting out of the Dornier's engines, at the same time that the plane dove for the ground. In his escape the German held for some time to the Vistula, after which he turned westward. Following the principles of the pursuit brigade, we went after the Dornier, which bolted with all its might, constantly increasing the distance between us. He became increasingly smaller until he finally disappeared into the checkerboard of fields and forests. So we broke off the pursuit and went back to our reconnaissance mission. Jaugsch nodded his head angrily. He had not yet experienced the bitter taste of his prize escaping from him in this unequal fight. My previous encounters had taught me to become indifferent. His disgusted, angry look amused me. I saw that he wanted to fight with the enemy at all costs, but that his Jedenastka, unfortunately, was too short-winded, not equal to the task.

We flew over a devastated Dęblin, and after a few minutes of flying along the bank of the Vistula we headed for home. The ground below us was a no-man's-land. I couldn't see any of our forces, nor any enemy movements. As we came upon Kazimierz, we descended to ground level and turned toward Bełżec. After landing I made a brief report of the course of the mission to the commander. Meanwhile, an angry Jaugsch emerged from the bushes. He was so irate that he completely ignored Karol trying to console him.

"Leon, take it easy, you look like a ghost. You've got blood all over your mouth? What did you do to yourself?" he admonished.

"To hell with my mouth! Damn Krauts! They made complete fools out of us, they escaped . . . as if nothing had happened!"

"Next time you'll get 'em," said Karol with a weak, feigned laugh. "And now wipe your face."

"Man, he's bullheaded," he turned to us. "Look how he's bitten his own lip in anger!"

"Why don't you send him on more missions, Wacek, at least he'll be a pleasant addition!"

"More jokes!" said Jaugsch indignantly.

"Don't take the joking seriously," said Karol. "That's one of the few things we've got left."

CHAPTER ELEVEN

Night Flight

AT NOON THE KRAKOWSKI SQUADRON AND THE WARSAW GROUP TOOK off for the new base. For us the order meant that we would have to prepare to leave Bełżec. The rumors continued to circulate that the Germans had crossed the Vistula and weren't far away. The situation wasn't a very pleasant one: waiting to leave while the enemy is on the way. The hours dragged on unbearably. In the tense atmosphere everyone felt extremely anxious and impatient.

Finally the sun went down behind the forest, casting its last rays before falling below the horizon. We were convinced that we wouldn't be flying anywhere this day, because it would be less than an hour before it would be completely dark.

"Somebody really screwed up! They must be real blockheads. Couldn't we have left with the others before dusk?" I could hear people saying.

The appearance of a car coming in our direction cheered us up a bit, however. After a short discussion with the colonel, our commander ordered the immediate withdrawal of the remaining column, leaving only one truck behind with the mechanics to prepare the planes for flight. Tadeusz was dejected. Within a few sentences he announced the new location, and instructions in case there was trouble in finding a new airfield. We quickly figured out the course and the time it would take to fly to Ostrożec near Łuck.

"Big talk!" said someone ironically.

"We won't be able to manage this before nightfall," said Tadeusz. "If need be we'll land at the airfield in Łuck."

Everything was done with lightning speed. As we had been informed, the Germans were advancing on us. Every minute was valuable. We had to evacuate the area as fast as we could, especially for the sake of our column of vehicles.

All the planes were already circling in the air and waiting for me to take off, but I couldn't get my engine started. Despite the efforts of our skilled mechanics, it wouldn't budge. So the group left without me. Beads of sweat began to form on my brow when I realized that I might be left there alone. And the silence and loneliness only increased my fear that something was happening in the area, and that the enemy might appear at any moment. The mechanics did everything possible to start my engine. Finally, it gasped and sputtered. The blades of the propeller spun around a couple of times and the engine began to turn. I let out a sigh of relief.

"Let us fill your tank, lieutenant!" shouted one of the mechanics.

"Don't have time for that!" I replied. "I've got to make up for lost time: fifteen minutes! It's warming up."

I waved goodbye and was off into the air. For a while I circled above the truck that was driving on the field path toward the road, because I wanted to give it an escort in case Germans showed up somewhere.

My compass dial whirled around, pointing in a southeasterly direction. The sky was already completely gray. Nevertheless, I descended to ground level to make it easier to see the planes of our group, whose route I was following, against the luminous clouds. It wasn't until I reached Hrubieszów that I saw the silhouettes of the Jedenastkas. They were flying in tight formation. I caught up with them and assumed the rear position. Dusk turned into night and one after another the silhouettes of the planes disappeared into the impenetrable darkness.

While in flight I continually counted the planes ahead of me. There were eleven of them. We were flying rather low along the Kowel-Łuck road when I suddenly noticed I was flying by myself. There was no one ahead of me. Nor could I see anything against the dark sky or the pitch-black ground. Everything dissolved into a murky abyss. Desperately I strained my eyes, only to confirm that I couldn't see anyone. So I decided to stay along the road, which I thought should take me to the new base. I also cut my throttle out of fear of crashing into someone. After all, all planes were supposed to follow the same course, and if the formation was dispersed, collisions might occur. I was also continually on the lookout for obstacles because it seemed that someone was constantly right ahead of me. After some time I noticed the bright ribbon of the Styr, alongside which I could, with difficulty, distinguish the gray mass of the crowded buildings of Łuck.

Knowing the position of the airfield, I cut across the city and found myself above it. Everything was pitch-black. There wasn't a light or a fire in sight. A disturbing thought crossed my mind: "Maybe the airfield's been captured?" That's all I would need.

Making a turn above it I decided to land. One way or another I had to come down. Landing on an unfamiliar field would only make things riskier.

I approached from the most suitable direction, from over the railroad tracks. As I remembered the airfield's surroundings from earlier times, there was a wooded cemetery on one side, a park on the second, and high office buildings on the third. Thus that left only the fourth and final direction of approach.

I could see the railroad tracks gleaming right below me. The lower I descended the denser the fog became, and the blinder I got. My plane drifted for a little while, after which I felt the ground. My plane tossed to and fro as it circled around wildly. I hit the brakes as hard as I could in fear of running into bomb craters.

Suddenly, like a specter, a dark form flashed right in front of me. I managed to notice only the flame issuing from its exhaust pipe. We didn't know it, but at that very moment we had had a brush with death because we had landed opposite each other in the pitch darkness. I didn't have time to think about it because at any moment someone else might land right on top of me. Nonetheless, I felt a great relief and exhaustion at the same time.

I hit the throttle and rolled out of danger, heading for one of the hangars that were still almost invisible in the dark, navigating solely on the basis of my recollection of the airfield. Overhead some plane buzzed me again. "Quite a nocturnal jamboree," I thought to myself. "Brings to mind the underworld."

Someone came out and kindly guided me with a lantern so that I'd know which way to go. A moment later I shut off my engine. Only then did I relax in my seat, congratulating myself. Again a shiver ran down the small of my back as I jumped out of my plane.

An indescribable turmoil, however, abounded in the darkness. Human shadows were running all around, calling out to one another. Names cascaded from every direction. I eagerly joined in this odd chorus of calls with all my might: "Tadeusz! Marian!" And when I got no answers: "Where's Toruń?"

This last method produced better results. I found everyone, except for Wilczewski, Pniak, and Czapiewski, who were still missing. They hadn't landed in Łuck, but probably found the airfield in Ostrożec about 12 kilometers away.

"Anyone make their landing approach from over the city?" I asked.

"I did," replied Marian.

"So we were the ones who just missed hitting each other?" I said with a smile.

"You can smile now, but at the time it didn't seem so funny!"

"At least we might have illuminated the other airfield for landing."

"Damn!" cursed Tadeusz. "Incompetence! And when you bring this to someone's attention all you get is a 'those are your orders!' To have to find—in the dark—some unknown, little field in Ostrożec that isn't even on the map. As if there wasn't time to move during the day."

"It's a disgraceful waste of human life," Marian chimed in. "And yet they ask us to make more sacrifices. Haven't we made enough already?"

"Unfortunately, there's nothing we can do about it. There are those who give the orders—which are not always the wisest—and those who have to carry them out," concluded Tadeusz. "Words are useless. We had better go look for lodgings in the barracks. Tomorrow at dawn we'll have to get out of here. There's so many of us here that it'll surely attract the attention of the Germans."

In fact there was an exceptionally large number of different types of aircraft at the airfield.

Knowing the airfield well, I led my colleagues to the main block of barracks where the group commander resided. In no time we found ourselves among a large crowd of pilots and observers, officers from all different groups whom fate had brought together in this one spot. Ragged units from almost all sectors of the front were brought here deep in the rear. The only exception was the Poznań group, whose squadrons remained with their army.

After the defeat that the main Polish forces suffered at the bend of the Vistula, the entire country was faced with final catastrophe. Our defense was torn to shreds, and lost what was left of its capacity to resist the smashing blows of the enemy. But despite the defeat, a tenacious, unequal struggle persisted. No one asked about the cost.

At dawn the airfield at Łuck echoed with the roar of engines warming up. With the first rays of the rising sun poking through the thick clouds of morning fog, we took off for Ostrożec. From above, the airfield at Łuck presented a picture of enormous chaos. The thick tangle of planes of different types parked close together would have been an exceptionally easy and attractive target for bombers. Some planes were still creeping along slowly toward takeoff, hoping to escape, as I already had, from this dangerous place. After a few minutes of flying, we separated for landing. Below us lay the country-estate of Count Ledóchowski in Ostrożec, on whose field lay a burned-out Jedenastka.

"We're here!" sighed Marian in relief, removing his helmet. "Yes, yes, that's the mansion ahead . . . maybe they can put together something for us to eat?"

The count received us *jako tako*—lukewarmly. Supposedly welcome, we were still made to feel as if we were undesired intruders. This didn't turn out bad in the end, but it could have been better.

Shortly thereafter Wacek Wilczewski flew in. The night before he had landed on a nearby potato field, which he came upon by chance. And despite the darkness he landed alongside the furrows, fortunately avoiding an unpleasant accident. He spent the night with the local farmer who received him very warmly. In the morning volunteers helped him drag his plane to a nearby field and take off without any loss.

"Know anything about Karol and Jasiu?" I asked Tadek delicately. "They must have landed somewhere in the vicinity."

"I thought they were already here," explained Wacek, excited by his extraordinary, nighttime adventure.

While Wacek entertained us with his story, Lieutenant Słonski, who had already been attached to us for some time, flew in from Łuck. Karol also showed up—with a broken leg and a swollen face. He had gotten a lift back from Młynów in a car. And Janek rode in on a peasant cart, proudly holding the reins in his hands.

The nocturnal jamboree of the crash victims dispelled our fears about their fate. Our "ingenious," nocturnal cross-country flight ended in the crash of two planes and Karol's broken leg. As we had anticipated, the airfield at Łuck was bombed by the Germans in the morning.

"They came over at about eight o'clock. Lots of people were killed, dammit!" said Słon. "Especially in the barracks. The field itself wasn't hit too badly. Only a few of the planes were destroyed. Our antiaircraft really had a time of it! Before the raid a Dornier-215, flying at about 2,000 meters, suddenly appeared over the field. Our artillery sent up an intense fire, but it was slow. All its bursts exploded behind the German, and he took off. Not fifteen minutes later one of our own bombers appeared over the field, flying along the same route and practically at the same altitude. Naturally, unable to distinguish the plane's silhouette, everyone started to fire at it, and it was hit right away. Damn them! At least the crew was able to bail out."

"You have to develop a nose for it," sighed Marian. "You have to learn to sense that something's wrong before the first bombs begin to fall! The next time we'll be able to take shelter in time."

"And how do your planes look?" Tadeusz asked Karol and Janek. "Maybe we'll be able to tell you when the ground crew arrives. Perhaps we'll be able to put one good plane together out of the parts of the two . . .," he mused out loud.

Karol sat on the ground dejected. Janek, although not physically hurt, was clearly discouraged too. He spoke first.

"All for nothing. Mine's lying on its back. Fuselage twisted, tail broken, wings seriously damaged too . . . it'll have to be repaired in a workshop! I thought," he said dolefully, "that the landing would be easy. But at the end of the runway I fell into a ditch. And of course, I fell in up to my nose . . ."

"Karol next!" laughed Wacek. "Tell us! So you were flying around and . . . what did you see?"

"I was flying along quietly, flying and . . . I didn't see anything," Karol mumbled through his swollen lips.

"And did you still have fuel for much longer?" I interrupted, because Karol was still talking about his flight, and we were more interested in his landing.

He looked at me disdainfully.

"Give me time, Stasiu, I'll still manage to crash . . ."

He was clearly displeased.

"So," he returned to his story, "I caught sight of this road below me, and flew alongside it for a while. I had no idea where I was, but I knew that it's always safer to stay with the roads. Help always arrives faster, and you'll never starve if something should happen to you. Eventually I thought to myself, 'You're out of fuel, there's nothing else to do, Karol, you're gonna have to land.' If there was a little more gas, I could've stayed up longer. 'But unfortunately they don't provide us with this necessity,' was the explanation. Only the kindly Countess Chodkiewiczowa offered me something . . ."

"You stayed at the Chodkiewiczes?" I interrupted.

"Yes, my dear Stasiu, near your beloved 'Dupno,'" he said, referring to my family's village, mispronouncing one of the syllables.

"That's Dubno with a B, Karol," I corrected him.

"Actually, it would have been better if you had been on this mission instead of me," he sighed. "It would have been easier for you if you had crashed near your home. The field I chose to land on looked frozen, shining against the background. I decided that it was the best I could do under the circumstances. And I'd be lucky if I'd be able to tell in the damned darkness that I was landing on a fairly level field. My plane could still crash, I thought to myself, as I banged the wheels on the ground at an angle. Even now it's all confusing. I mishandled it horribly. My plane somersaulted, I don't know how many times. And anyway, in the darkness there was no way to know . . . I finally came to rest, as it turns out, upside down on a ploughed field. The field was made of clay, and that's why it appeared shiny at night. There was a mess in the cockpit. Dust and dirt everywhere! Suddenly I banged my head on something hard and lost consciousness, but only for a little while. When I came to I climbed out of the demolished plane like a fox out of its den . . . and then went looking for people. I could feel blood on my face. It was only when I reached the mansion, or what there was left of it, that I saw human faces. The old woman, who turned out to be Countess Chodkiewiczowa, was quite frightened. I looked in the mirror myself and was unpleasantly surprised. My entire face, can you imagine, was plastered with mud and bleeding. Damn him!" he concluded with this pleasant invocation. "The genius who came up with this idea ought to be sent out at night himself! Let him try to find a place to land in unknown territory. Then he might be more careful about the fate of those who have to follow his orders."

In the meantime the wing commander arrived with new orders directing the group not to the east, since there was no place to go there, nor to the south, since there wasn't time, but to the northwest, to Kutno, where, since the previous day, the Poznań and Pomorze armies had been waging a heavy battle with overwhelming enemy forces. The mission was to reinforce the solitary and reduced Poznań group by providing air cover for our armies fighting there. The order filtered down the normal channels to the commanders of the units that had to carry out the order. But our operational "geniuses"—for whom there were no obstacles—did not take the least trouble to consider whether the mission could be performed at all. "Range—they certainly must have thought—is no matter of concern. They'll have to fly there on empty tanks, because that's the order." The landing field—who cares? Anywhere around Kutno. Fuel, ammunition, ground crews—all these "trivialities" were never taken into consideration. Only a lack of the most elementary understanding of the facts could produce such a backward rationale.

Our commanders who received these unrealistic orders, which were improvised without the least understanding of the mission, had to fight—as prudently as possible—with their immediate superiors, showing them the irrationality of the orders and the impossibility of executing them. As usual, our commander showed judgment and energy. Eventually the colonel was convinced, and agreed with Tadeusz's plan to fly to Kutno with a stop in Brześć [Brest] (on the Bug River) where the group could be refueled and received detailed information from General Headquarters about the location of the Poznań group. The group's ground crew, however, which always lagged behind in the course of evacuations—and without which we were constantly powerless—had to be directed to Kutno immediately upon arrival in Ostrożec.

The "Warsaw people" quickly gave us some fuel and without further ado we took off for Brześć.

CHAPTER TWELVE

Chaos

FOR THE FIRST TIME IN THE COURSE OF THE WAR, THE WEATHER WAS bad. There was drizzle, and low-lying clouds stretched far to the north. We flew over an enormous airfield that had been prepared for French bombers. According to the stipulations of the military treaty, the French were to take off from their own bases, bomb the eastern industrial region of the Reich, and land in Poland.

The airfield was half-empty.

We landed under an overcast sky at the field at Brześć, which had suffered severely from bombing. The sides of the hangar there had been blown out from end to end. Immediately upon landing Tadeusz took a motorcycle over to the fortified headquarters. We were to be used as immediate reinforcements. Each of us had to go get gas and roll his own 3-liter gas can across the entire airfield to his plane. We rolled our cans along to the strains of *burłak* [Russian riverboat haulers] songs. When we had reached the middle of the field, seven Dornier-17s popped out of the clouds to distract us. All we could do was drop our gas cans and run when we heard the antiaircraft open fire. Fortunately our fire was accurate. One plane was hit and the rest, not wanting to break up their formation, jumped back into the clouds.

The absence of our commander dragged on, and we were already impatient because we thought it might mean a repetition of our nocturnal escapade, even more so because the overclouding brought the darkness on earlier.

While we were pondering our situation, we could begin to hear the sound of an approaching plane. It wasn't too far off, but we couldn't see it yet. There wasn't time or the possibility of taking shelter, so we ran to a nearby cabbage field and hit the ground. Stach Zieliński, however, lost his head for a moment and ran to a nearby toilet and meticulously closed the doors. Instead of an expected enemy plane, however, it turned out to be a Polish Lockheed passenger airliner heading south. Wacek expressed genuine regret at this because he couldn't control his curiosity about what Zieliński would have done if it had been an enemy bombing raid. Zieliński, however, wasn't in a hurry to explain.

It was already dark when Tadeusz showed up, telling us that we would be leaving the next day. Of course, not for Kutno, but for Ostrożec. A return . . . this was a bit too much for us. We couldn't restrain ourselves.

"What crap . . . ! For several days now we've been flying from place to place like lunatics," we complained.

"In addition," he continued, "I would like to inform you that the Germans are already closing in on Brześć. So we'll have to be alert because the devil never sleeps. . . ."

We began to look for a place to stay for the night close to our planes. The most suitable spot turned out to be the cottage of a local worker who greeted us with hitherto unencountered cordiality. He put together a meal for us from his meager provisions and sympathized with our plight. And not only did he not accept any payment from us, but he considered it the highest honor to let us stay with him. In the morning, as we were leaving, we left some money on the table. It may not have been the best way to thank him, but we didn't need the money and we thought it might help him.

Below us stretched the dreary, monotonous Polesian landscape: pastures, meadows, and bogs; as far as the eye could see, a monotonous, unending plain. The endless line of the railroad tracks meandered back and forth across our path toward Ostrożec. The war hadn't yet reached this part of the country. Only its advanced parties had visited. So far the targets had been only bridges and train stations. Some bridges over the Pripet and Stochód had not been destroyed, although bomb craters were visible alongside them. Waving arms rose up to greet us as we flew low over the sparsely strewn, simple villages.

After flying for some time, I noticed a large lake ahead. I thereupon moved to the right wing of the formation. I wasn't ready to take a bath if my engine decided to conk out on me, which was a real possibility at any moment, considering my plane's condition. When I got up alongside Marian, he laughed at my "maneuver," undoubtedly guessing its reason. In the meantime my engine ran flawlessly. And its tranquil, monotonous drone helped to calm my frazzled nerves. The breeze coming into the cockpit invigorated me too.

Nothing remained of the morning fog. The sun climbed higher in the sky, indicating a sunny day and eradicating the sign of a change in the weather. Such a sign contained, after all, the seeds of hope that at least nature would effectively resist the Germans.

We reached Łuck by turning at Ostrożec. Wacek had to remain in Brześć because he couldn't get his engine started. After landing we learned that our ground crew had managed in the meantime to reach Kutno that morning. An Erwudziak was sent out immediately. It found and recognized our transport on the Kowel road. It landed on a convenient nearby field and thus rescued it for the unit.

From an operational point of view, our activity slowly began to be reduced to zero. There had been no conception of the proper use of air units in combat. Clearly there was no understanding that the lack of fuel had become our main problem and that leaving it unsolved completely excluded the possibility of our continued participation in the war. Disorganization in the rear also became severe and resupply ceased to exist.

The group commander, who was by no means required to do so, took it upon himself to leave the unit and look for fuel, which we needed at any cost. Despite enormous difficulties and the clear incompetence of our upper-level command, who fell in stature and trust with every passing day, the martial spirit and deep feeling of responsibility that we had on the first day of the war remained intact. We were discouraged, but not broken. Direct communication with the front had been destroyed, which also discouraged us. Bored by inactivity, we lay under our planes in anticipation of some sudden change, of a reversal of the clock, which in the meantime relentlessly measured out the painful events for us.

Around noon Wacław returned from Brześć, and along with him came five planes from the 151st Squadron in Wilno [Vilnius] under the command of Lieutenant Woliński. Five planes and five pilots—nothing more. They had no idea where their ground crew was and had recently been roaming around without it. Under these conditions Woliński had decided to attach their squadron to ours. This was the only option because they still constituted a solid unit, and the idea of a guerrilla war in the air was unrealistic.

Woliński was accompanied by a friend of mine from my Dęblin training school days, Jan Bury-Burzymski, who was called the "seal" because of his swimming prowess. After greeting each other we began to exchange opinions about the last few days. In doing so, the seal sketched a picture of his group commander with his usual sarcasm.

"He decided," Jan exploded with indignation, "to command from the ground because he thought that he was too valuable to jeopardize himself in the air! And all of this might have passed without much notice if it wasn't for the fact that the last time anyone saw our 'commander' was as he got into his car at the end of August. Since then there's been no trace of him. It seems the storms of war have precluded our intrepid genius from demonstrating his talents in commanding the group from the ground."

During the course of our conversation, a vehicle with our ground crew drove up into the farm-yard of the estate, having fortunately returned from its futile trip to Kutno. Upon arrival the language of the crew left no doubt that they were all fed up with this pointless and absurd traveling back and forth. The men, worn-out by the trip, wasted on fighting their way through in different kinds of vehicles headed in all directions, lay down next to one another. Fortunately they had experienced no losses in men or matériel.

"Any gas left in the cars?" I asked the crew chief.

"Not much," he replied, "Maybe two or three of them have some . . ."

"Then why don't you put that in my plane, as soon as you've had a chance to get some rest," I requested.

At this, Wacek jumped all over me.

"What are you up to?!"

"I want a full tank," I said. "We might meet a patrol. After all, the Germans are active in this area too."

"What! In this mess? Where are you going to fly. We have no intelligence and I don't think we'll get any!"

"Still it's not that bad," I consoled him. "It looks worse than it is. We're still in good shape, and can hold out till winter!"

"A joke's a joke," he said, "but the situation is beginning to scare me. I'm afraid that we don't have much time left. Hell, I just managed to get out of Brześć at the last moment. At this rate if the Germans push any farther it won't be long before we'll have to get out of here. Where to then?"

I didn't want to give up my optimism.

"We can still go north," I said. "That way's still open."

"And then what?" he pressed me.

"Take it easy, Wacek, you're looking on the bad side. You count your winnings only after you leave the table. The game isn't over yet. And our cards might still change. . . ."

We concluded our conversation and I persuaded Wacek to help the exhausted crew refuel the planes. After refueling a few of them the mechanics went back to rest, when suddenly from behind the trees we could hear the roar of engines. Three Dornier-17s popped out flying along the Łuck-Dubno road.

"Wacek!" I shouted, "What do you think?"

"Okay, let's go!"

The Dorniers flew very close to us, firing at the road from treetop level. But before I could start my engine they had disappeared over the misty horizon.

I continued to fly above the road thinking that I'd meet them on their way back rather than try to go after them. Before Dubno I jumped up to 500 meters to get a better look, but visibility was limited by the smoke covering the entire area. This corner of the country, in which it would be difficult to find a factory chimney, now looked like a great industrial center. As I could see, the train station in Dubno had also received its share of bombing. Searching for the Dorniers' trail, I changed my course toward Krzemieniec. The wooden houses in the center of the town were burning like torches. The broken-down hovels of the impoverished Jews obviously constituted "an important military objective" for the Luftwaffe. Hitler had unleashed this terror from the air to break the people's spirit of resistance. After circling the town a couple of times, I started on my way back. I was seized by dejection. I began to ask myself desperate questions: "Can't anything be done? Why are we so weak, who is to blame, and can anyone be blamed?" The questions spun around in my head, but I couldn't find any answers to them. At the time I didn't know enough.

I left behind me the floodwaters of the Ikwa, Dubno, and Młynów—the area where I had grown up. I skimmed the surface of the field and my Jedenastka rolled along the ground, rocking on its sides in the last phase of the landing.

"How'd you do?" I asked Wacek as I switched off my engine. "Get any of 'em?"

"Naah!" he shrugged his shoulders. "It was hopeless, a waste of fuel. It's only an accident when you encounter an enemy plane."

This time we had switched places. Wacek laughed at my dejection. He was happy that we could still fly, if only Tadeusz could find the fuel.

For the time being we could only do one thing—wait.

We waited for a long time for the return of "the old man" who turned up in Ostrożec only in the late evening dirty and exhausted. His search yielded nothing. Aviation fuel was nowhere to be found. We were threatened with complete "operational death." During the course of lively evening debates over this problem, someone brought up the possibility of using the gas in the cars. But Tadeusz didn't give in and announced another search expedition for the next day.

"Tomorrow I'll go to Kiwerc and try my luck," he said. "Since it has a train station it's possible that at least one tank car might still be left there. If we have no luck with that then we'll have to try the automobile fuel. The only question is: How will our engines react to the change?"

Paweł, who was a kind of expert in this area, assured us that the engines wouldn't conk out on us but added at the same time that with automobile fuel they wouldn't attain the power that high-octane aviation fuel provides.

"Tomorrow we'll have to talk with the mechanics about it," Tadeusz concluded.

The next day right after breakfast the count very delicately requested that we might want to move our belongings into the farm buildings on his estate. It seemed that the rooms we were occupying had been reserved for the minister of military affairs, General Kasprzycki, and his staff. There was nothing we could do but acquiesce to his request. To be sure, the general's staff didn't seem to be so large that it would require the entire place. But apparently reasons of state excluded his staying in the exclusive company of spirited flying personnel, even more so since his staff included a person under "special custody"—a certain Miss Kajzerówna.[1]

After winning the first battle with little difficulty, the count moved on to the next request, which was a bit more ticklish. It seemed that the count sincerely sympathized with us about the unsuitability of the landing field on his estate. And in connection with that he suggested that we move to another field. Wanting to help us as much as possible, he kindly suggested the Jezierski estate a few kilometers away where there was a splendid, large field that was much more suitable to our purposes than his rocky field.

But the truth will always come out. The count explained that his racing horses were spooked by the roar of our engines, and our presence also created the danger of becoming a target for bombers.

"You understand . . . ," he concluded with a courteous smile.

Tadeusz nervously smoked one cigarette after another. But he was able to control himself and remained extremely polite to the end. We

---

[1] Translator's note: Zofia Kajzerówna was an actress with whom General Tadeusz Kasprzycki was having an affair. In the spring of 1939 this affair was the cause of the suicide of Kasprzycki's wife and the consequent estrangement of his son. Kasprzycki escaped to Romania in 1939, and from there petitioned the Sikorski government for a position in the Polish army in the West. This petition was rejected on the basis of his complete incompetence and responsibility for failing to prepare the army for combat in 1939.

glanced at one another during this entire episode clenching our teeth so that we wouldn't explode. When the count became insistent, I couldn't contain myself.

"After all, we have to make a stand somewhere!" I bellowed. "Whether here or somewhere else, it's all the same to us, and not our choice. You'll remember us and be mighty sorry when the next people get here. And the Germans are better behaved than we . . . I hope that you won't have to be convinced of this yourself."

The count diplomatically left. We remained by ourselves, packing up our meager belongings. Tadeusz, after giving the orders to the squadron commanders, wasted no time in setting out for Kiwerc.

Under these exceptional circumstances Captain Tadeusz Rolski proved to be an exceptional commander. He participated in combat missions, and, in addition, shouldered the heavy burden of the fate of the entire unit and the preservation of its combat capability. Working during the day, he spent many a night traveling to staff headquarters. As difficulties piled up with every passing day, the unit was increasingly faced with a "lack of necessities." Tadeusz never refused a helping hand. He never lacked energy, did what he could, and was always ready to dig up the means necessary to guarantee the possibility of continuing the fight. Although a bit despotic, his demeanor and care for people earned him the complete trust and profound friendship of his subordinates.

Around noon a favorable sky allowed us to catch a glimpse of our "little friends." The minister and his companion were carefully avoiding open spaces. I am sure it was less out of protecting Miss Kajzerówna's complexion from the rays of the sun and the harshness of the wind than for "defense purposes," of concealing this romantic tête-à-tête of the minister of military affairs of a country at war against the eyes of enemy aircraft. With understanding and admiration I tipped my cap to the discrimination of our astute commander who had decided not to be surprised. After all, stripes on the trousers really might attract the enemy's attention.

Paweł, as usual inelegantly and without an appreciation of the gravity and temper of the moment, burst out laughing.

"Look, the general's instructing his sweetheart. A future 'pilot.'"

"The minister spends his time agreeably, and at the same time with great advantage to the country," I corrected him. "Can't you tell from his face how he is planning to conquer Berlin? This serenity deserves admiration."

The two lovers vanished into the distance. It left us with a feeling of disgust and abhorrence.

We were concerned, however, by the news broadcast by the Wilno radio station that that evening our bombers had bombed Berlin. Such "false reports" could be accepted as true only by a public opinion that was completely ignorant of our air force's truly tragic situation, by a public opinion that had been systematically misled, and that believed the billboards proclaiming: "Strong, United, Ready!"

Our situation hadn't changed. Tadeusz's daylong efforts to find fuel met with no success, and the future looked even darker.

The night spent on straw beds didn't do anything for our appearance either. Upon arising we looked like scarecrows with stale blades of straw sticking in our hair. We couldn't help joking as we groomed ourselves.

"The minister really did a job on us," laughed the always cheerful Wacek. "And our noble host wasn't even kind enough to have fresh straw laid down for us. If he had come here with a couple of ministers, I suppose we'd have to move into the cow-barn."

We achieved a semblance of order and moved out for breakfast to the main "pavilion." In the meantime we had not even been invited to eat in . . . the barn.

It was the 13th of September, a day no different from the others—warm, clear, sunny—a truly golden autumn. Not much time had passed since the outbreak of war and the entire country had already fallen into ruin. And with the ruin collapsed all our hopes. It was difficult to come to terms with the inescapable prospect that the imminent future portended absolute defeat. We still retained eleventh-hour illusions however—against better judgment.

Since Władek Różycki urgently needed a dentist, I was given permission to accompany him to a specialist in Dubno and allowed to pay a visit to my parents at the same time. Our commander generously offered us his Chevy, and in the afternoon we took off. The Chevy ate up the kilometers. On the way we met a group of civilian guards with red and white armbands who controlled traffic along the roads. A half an hour later we arrived at our destination. The town was filled with activity. A large number of outsiders had fled the German advance to this—supposedly—distant rear supply depot. Dubno was swamped with ministries and national offices that had been evacuated, and all homes were filled to the brim with officials.

My parents were delighted to see me, but also surprised. I had to admit that the town was not the same as it was in its prewar days. And the people had a hard time adapting to the abrupt changes produced by the war. When I got to my parents' house, I felt relieved. When I was young it always seemed to be so safe that I thought nothing could disturb it. It was only in the course of the few hours I spent at home with my family that I fully came to realize and appreciate the meaning of the words *home, father, mother* . . . I really wanted to stay with them. Every now and then I would steal a glance at the clock. And if I could have held back time I certainly would have done so. Knowing glances at Władek, however, indicated that it was time to be on our way.

After tea we had to bid farewell, which I wanted to keep as brief as possible.

My father pressed his lips together tightly. He didn't say anything, and only with the greatest of effort was able to suppress his emotions. He put his powerful hand on my shoulder and whispered, "Fight for Poland to the end." This was the only testament he bequeathed me. My mother bid farewell to Władek and our driver as if they were her own sons.

My mother had a hard time controlling herself. I felt powerless and heartbroken when I had to pull myself delicately away from her.

On the street I was surrounded by a group of young girls who had come out specifically to see us. Among them was a former classmate of mine who kissed me goodbye. Eight years later I learned that the Nazis had killed her.

After returning to Ostrożec we were shattered by the news of Mirek's death, which was brought by a driver who had been attached to the group in our absence.

Evacuated from the hospital in Brześć, Mirek died of gangrene the same morning in Kowel. There seemed to be no indication that he was in such serious danger. During the course of the evacuation he was in high spirits, even flirted with his nurse, and was counting the days until he'd return to the group. A brilliant, but all too brief, chapter in the history of a fighter pilot had come to an unexpected end. Three victories in two encounters—unequal encounters, conducted against an enemy who enjoyed a colossal advantage. It's hard to explain to someone who hasn't gone through it himself. I don't think that there were any fighter pilots in the entire Second World War who fought under such difficult conditions as those experienced by the Polish fighter pilots in September 1939.

The number of planes destroyed—150—and an equal number damaged does not tell the whole story. Even the Germans admitted to much greater losses suffered in combat in the air war against Poland.

The history of the Polish air force shall forever be inscribed with the names of Leśniewski, Laskowski, Urban, Mielczyński, Medwecki, Okrzeja, and many others who during the tragic days of September 1939 paid the ultimate price in the defense of their country.

CHAPTER THIRTEEN

The Last Airfield

A LACK OF AVIATION FUEL FORCED US TO REFUEL OUR PLANES IN PART with gasoline from the cars. The group was then ready to make the announced base change. A column of cars was lined up underneath the trees, and we began to hope our period of inactivity would finally come to an end. The new orders directed us south to the vicinity of Litiatyn near Brzeżany, about 150 kilometers away. To be sure, we were a little perplexed as to why we were moving south and not west where the fighting was going on. And the absence of accurate information about the situation on the entire front precipitated different ideas. We didn't understand why the commander-in-chief wanted to use our units in the southern sector. But the announced concentration of all fighter planes in the Brzeżany region seemed to make some sense.

So we left Ostrożec for the south. After flying for about twenty minutes, we came upon the Podolian hills. The picturesque countryside was captivating. The air here was perfectly clear; the smoke from the fires of war hadn't yet reached this part of the country. At a certain spot the hills opened up and we entered onto a broad valley. Flying alongside a river that flowed south, we approached our destination. Keeping to one side of Brzeżany, we circled over the rim of the hills and came in for a landing one after the other. The narrow landing strip, which had slopes that on one side fell steeply into a deep ravine and on the other into a train trench, didn't appear very attractive from the air.

We arrived just as we had at our last base. The Krakowski group and the two Warsaw groups were on a neighboring hill, while the Lwów,

Wilno, and Toruń groups were represented on our ridge. This, for us, massive concentration produced a vigorous commotion only on the ground; activity in the air was limited to reconnaissance flights in the direction of Lwów by units that had arrived here earlier.

Suddenly three Dornier-17s appeared, flying low over the forest. They fired on the Krakowski and Warsaw groups but didn't cause any damage. One of the Dorniers was shot down by our antiaircraft guns, but none of its crew members was able to save himself.

Late in the day I took off with Wacek on a reconnaissance mission, turning west at 800 meters. After a little while we could see the mound of Unia Lubelska and Wysoki Zamek. We passed over Lwów and turned toward Gródek-Przemyśl, along the way attracting fire from some of our own disoriented infantry. When we entered enemy territory, we descended. Wacek made a wide turn in a northerly direction to cut across all local roads in search of German columns. But there was no enemy activity in our assigned region of patrol. Only anemic and inaccurate antiaircraft fire reminded us that we were flying over enemy-occupied territory. The Germans sought cover in the forests and undergrowth. Wacek then changed his course in a southeasterly direction, and we headed home. The sun was already going down when we landed in Litiatyn. I decided not to land on the top of the hill but on the slope like a glider. The slope was steep, with about a 45-degree angle, which forced me to maintain full speed since the deflection still continued for a little while. What a strange landing. Instead of the ground I saw the sky, with my feet upturned almost over my head. When I hit the ground, however, my plane was barely able to roll a few meters against the steep rise, completely running off the runway. I didn't expect such a short landing strip and so I hit the throttle in fear of tumbling down.

"I see you don't like to land where everyone else does!" joked Marian as I climbed out of my plane.

"Try it yourself tomorrow," I said, "and you'll see that it's safer than this narrow bump . . ."

"What! he landed on that hill?" asked Wacek incredulously. "What were you thinking of? Are you tired of living? If your engine had conked out, you would have flipped over so many times that we'd still be picking up parts of you and your plane."

"Take it easy, Wacek!" I said, "Why do you always look on the dark side of things?"

"That's enough!" interrupted Marian, turning toward Wacek. "We have to go down and find a place for the people who'll arrive tonight."

And so we headed off in the direction of the buildings at the bottom of the hill where arrangements had been made for us to stay in the house of a retired veteran. Wacek and Marian were faced with a difficult task, since all the houses had already been occupied by the other groups. I had to go with them to make sure I wouldn't be left out. Fortunately, group chauvinism had ceased to exist by this time and all the groups helped each other out. So the problem was eventually solved and everyone found a place to stay despite the limited accommodations. The Wilno and Lwów groups were crowded into three little rooms.

The local people greeted us warmly. They had decided everyone would have a place for the night, and that in the worst case scenario we would take turns sleeping.

"We're sure that there are poker players among you," they said, "so for those who want to go to sleep now there's enough places." This approach to the problem relieved our fears for the moment that there might not be enough room. We ate a very meager supper—which was supplemented by cigarettes—during which we exchanged opinions about the general situation. But none of these was based on factual knowledge. We still didn't know anything. None of us thought that we were going to lose the war. We thought we were just experiencing a temporary setback. The excitement of our discussions only took us further from reality.

The next morning we sent a team of buyers to Brzeżany to get a necessary assortment of clothing, the serious lack of which we were beginning to feel. This problem stemmed from another case of false optimism. None of us reckoned that we would be forced far from our home bases, and so we thought we would be able to go home from time to time and get the items we needed.

As luck would have it, none of the stores in Brzeżany had aviators' shirts or men's undergarments (we were looking for knee-length). The

Jewish shopkeeper admitted that these were out of season. But he said he had some exceptionally fine women's silk "panties." So Lieutenant Grzech, who had been ordered not to come back empty-handed, bought the panties, and some blue shirts that came closest to our uniforms. Some of the men sarcastically advised Grześ (which is what we called him) to work out instructions on how to put the panties on, because they already knew how to take them off. The silk panties, however, actually turned out to be very serviceable under field conditions.

I was walking up the hill to my plane when I saw a detachment of infantry emerge from out of the forest, making its way along the ravine toward Litiatyn. I noticed how exhausted they were by what I'm sure must have been for them a very long march. They probably had taken shortcuts, off the road, trying to avoid artillery while being constantly harassed from the air.

Their faces were tired and dirty, and I felt sorry for them as I stood there on the hill watching them for a long time as they passed by.

I finally got to the top of the hill where there was a great commotion. A flight had just taken off and two planes were coming in for a landing.

"What's up with them?" I asked Wacek, who was absorbed in a map.

"Patrol of Lwów and reconnaissance," he answered, not even looking up. "I'm glad you're here, though . . . want something to do?"

"What a question!" I said.

"Good! then we'll go out on patrol at noon."

"That's fine with me. Any other of our group flying?"

"Yeah, but they didn't encounter anything. The Germans apparently are now alternating with us. When we're in the air they're on the ground, and vice versa. This way we don't disrupt each other," he laughed. "Nice cooperation, huh?"

"And where're Tadek and Marian?" I asked him.

"Tadeusz went to a briefing, and Marian's out with Leszek on patrol. We'll go out when they get back."

The groups on the neighboring hill were busy too. Every now and then I could see a plane taking off to replace one that had just landed.

Suddenly from behind the forest a Jedenastka zipped by, and after circling, made his landing approach from above the ravine. The pilot landed on the side of the hill and not its top. The plane, handled nicely, gently plopped down on the top of the hill where the pilot quickly headed in our direction.

"Look!" I shouted to Wacek, "it's Marian. See what he did? Yesterday the bum got on my ass for doing the same thing! But still he had to try it himself!"

Marian waved to us as he taxied his plane into the bushes.

"And where's Leszek?" I asked Wacek. "Did they get him? He should have returned with Marian."

Marian climbed out of his plane, upset because he didn't know what had happened to his wingman.

"He simply disappeared into thin air," he declared. "I saw him during our first attack and then when I peeled off to return because I was out of ammunition, he wasn't there."

"What did you attack?" I interrupted impatiently.

"A German column. I don't think that they got him during our attack, although the fire from the ground was intense . . . I would have seen it if they did!"

"Do you think he has any gas left?" I asked.

Marian looked at his watch.

"He still has about a half an hour left, but not more . . . but it's already late."

"Where are the Germans?" asked Wacek. "Where did you attack them?"

Marian spread out the map.

"We found them on the open road, they had no place to hide . . ."

"And in the air anything?"

"Empty!" Marian shrugged his shoulders.

"No need to hurry to our planes, there's still time," said Wacek looking at his watch.

Our planes took off one after the other, and after briefly forming up with Corporal Klein, we headed off in a westerly direction. Patroling the assigned region at 2,000 meters, we didn't encounter any enemy activity in the air and I began to get bored with the "sweep." Wacek shook his head as if to acknowledge that it wasn't his fault that there were no Germans around. To be sure, for those on the ground this was rather nice, but on the other hand it would have been better had German planes been flying while we were on patrol.

Wacek made a sharp turn and headed home. Once again we returned empty-handed. On the way I was careless and didn't pay attention to where I was flying. If I had had to return alone, I would have been in trouble. The time passed quickly, and I didn't even notice when Wacek dipped his wings to indicate that we should break up for our landing approaches.

After landing I saw Leszek among the pilots. "He finally got back," I thought to myself. As it turned out Leszek simply lost Marian and wandered around on his return. He landed on a convenient field far to the east of Brzeżany. It was only then that I realized how close the Russian border was.

"You could have gone a little farther," laughed Wacek. "When you got to Kijów [Kiev] you would have known where you were."

"Next time I'll try it," Leszek promised.

At supper we learned that Stach Zatorski of the Warsaw group was missing. He had gone out early in the morning and had not returned.

Unconfirmed rumors began to spread that there was going to be a reorganization and a group of pilots would be sent to pick up new British and French planes. The news excited us, and everyone imagined that his group would be the first to be equipped with the new planes.

Tadeusz divulged nothing, although we suspected he had already been informed about the changes to come. From time to time he glanced at a letter, and this only confirmed our belief that something was up and that the rumors "had legs." We had to wait patiently however, for the last card to be played.

Around three o'clock Corporal Wieprzkowicz and I took off on a reconnaissance flight. After flying past Lwów we descended to treetop level heading along our assigned route. Our assignment was to reconnoiter all the roads leading to Lwów. Weaving through enemy territory

I stayed beneath the trees to protect myself from the sharp eyes of German observers. The road that we followed led for a little way through a forest.

A few minutes later we came out into the open. In a valley I could see a long column of cavalry on the march. The similarity between their cavalry uniforms and our flying uniforms was so striking that at first I thought it must be one of our units. But the helmets gave them away! The Germans instantly scattered, fleeing into every break in the terrain and the nearby underbrush. But we were able to bring fire on the largest part of them, hitting many. We repeated our attacks until we exhausted our ammunition.

The Germans quickly organized a defense though, and a duel began between their machine-gun positions and us. Their defensive positions weren't active for long, however. Hardly would one open up than it would have us on its back. With short bursts I fired on small groups of cavalry soldiers lying along the ditches. When we were out of ammunition we had to stop, and we took off in an easterly direction. As we went we could see riderless horses running along the fields.

When a few minutes later we had reached a safer area, I climbed to get a better view of our position. One thousand meters to one side I could see Lwów, which meant that I had to correct my course and turn more to the south. This time I stuck to the map, remembering what had happened to Leszek that morning. Wieprzkowicz was alongside me, smiling that we would at least return with our guns empty.

The lake at Brzeżany glistened in the rays of the sun. Below us the railway line twisted through the mountains, and on the left lay the airfield.

"We're still waiting for Stach," said Wacek while finishing his report on the reconnaissance mission.

Not long after, two Jedenastkas appeared against the graying sky, coming in our direction.

"They've returned," sighed Wacek with relief.

The planes, in the meantime, started their landing approaches, but over the opposite hill. They weren't ours.

We were still standing on the edge of the forest, looking toward the west as time ran out, and there was no plane in sight. Suddenly we could hear the roar of engines and from behind the hill two Jedenastkas shot up in a chandelle together.

Darkness was falling by the time we left the hill.

"Where are the damned krauts?" asked Stach Zieliński angrily. "I didn't see one all day. They've got to be flying too! I bet that they've been transferred west?!"

"Maybe they're operating in other directions," I interjected, "and we can't venture too far . . ."

"What's with our 'Napoleon'?" asked Stach, changing the subject. "He's pissed off; did you try to get something out of him?"

"He's as quiet as the sphinx," said Marian, "pretending he doesn't know anything. We'll need to soften him up a bit. Maybe he'll give in and reveal something."

Our attempts met with no success. Tadeusz always changed the topic, trying to skirt the issue. But he remained angry.

From early morning of the 16th of September, it was relatively quiet on both hills. Only the roar of engines warming up upset the general calm. No planes, however, were sent out on missions.

The mechanics poked around in the engines, and the pilots, bored with their inactivity, lay in their flying suits at the edge of the forest, warming themselves in the sun.

Something hung in the air, however. The hours passed leisurely by, and the sun had reached its zenith before the anticipated bombshell finally came.

We were called to a briefing. The group commander explained the newly devised plan. A complete reorganization of fighter forces was to follow. The group was to be transformed into one squadron, under the command of Lieutenant Słonski, and was to remain in place and be included within another, mixed group. However, the majority of the advanced combat pilots and experienced mechanics were to leave by car for Czernowiec, Romania, to pick up new fighters: British Hurricanes and French Morane-406s.

These planes, purchased by Poland before the war, had come by sea to Gdynia. In the first days of the war, they were withdrawn to northern Denmark and taken by a circuitous route over the Mediterranean Sea to Romania, which was Poland's ally.

I was happy to be attached to the group leaving for Romania. Within a few hours of the announcement, a column was formed and ready to go. Marian and Wacek took the lead as navigators and Tadeusz, as commander of the entire group, brought up the rear of the column in his Chevy, and we headed out on the shortest route for Śniatyn.

During the first hours, in daylight, we moved along nicely. But from the moment that darkness fell the trip became a real ordeal. The cars moved as slowly as ghosts, constantly braking so as not to run into one another. After a few hours of traveling in the dark, our navigators got lost and didn't recognize anything. Around eleven o'clock at night we stopped in some out-of-the-way place, a bakery that was working all night for the army. The smell of fresh bread was delicious and whetted our appetites, and the bread that we bought disappeared into our stomachs in no time. After a brief rest for our drivers, we started out again.

After midnight, when we had gotten ourselves straightened out again, we could see a lamp flickering ahead of us in the dark. It was a signal to stop the cars. We drove up slowly, and our driver got out. When I got out of the car, someone I couldn't quite see immediately began to yell at the pilots, and then at me in particular.

"You've destroyed state property!" roared the agitated voice of a captain—if I saw his insignia properly. "You've thrown bombs worth their weight in gold into the ditch! I order you to load them immediately back onto your car."

I listened incomprehensively to this verbal explosion. "Bombs?" I asked incredulously. "We've got nothing to do with bombs, Captain. Are you sure they're bombs?"

"Of course!" he replied.

He ordered me to accompany him to the ditch beside the road and shined his lamp on some shattered cases, but they contained no bombs. To support his claim he drew his pistol, threatening to use it if I didn't comply with his order.

Indignantly I held my breath.

"I'd like to know since when have infantry rifles become aerial bombs. I am surprised that you, a commissioned infantry officer, cannot tell the difference between aerial bombs and your own army's rifles. Anyway, if they were bombs we couldn't load them on our car because it's already loaded with radio equipment. In addition, I have my own orders and can disregard yours or anyone else's," I said.

In the meantime another truck drove up and a bunch of mechanics got out. The captain, seeing that the situation was becoming complicated, quickly put away his gun and requested my papers. There was a brief exchange of authorizations after which we moved on.

Less than half an hour later we were forced to stop by another lantern.

"I guess some idiot is gonna jerk us around about bombs again?" said platoon leader Dembkowski as he stopped the car.

By their voices I recognized they were friendlies. It seems that a large truck, which before the war must have been used to move furniture, had fallen into a ditch and that it was only by luck, thanks to the fact that it was going slowly, that the people inside had escaped injury and the truck itself wasn't badly damaged. It took us almost two hours to pull it out of that trap.

We were slowed even more by the exhaustion of our drivers, who had to watch very carefully so as not to run off the road into ditches. By dawn our engine began to cough and finally quit on us. Our leader drove up alongside us. We had to find the cause of the problem. The cars behind us came to a stop and offered to help, but our driver was too proud and said that he could handle it himself.

Finally Tadeusz, our "commander," came by. He decided to slow the column down so as to give us a chance to catch up with them as soon as we got the problem fixed. I was sleepy, exhausted by the trip, and since I couldn't help in fixing the engine I decided to take a nap in a nearby secluded mountaineer's cabin.

The cabin's owner welcomed me and before long I was asleep on a large, firm bed.

Tadeusz, who returned with a rope an hour later to take us in tow, woke me up and we finally caught up with the group which was waiting in Horodenka.

During the entire night our navigators had not made one mistake. Now, in daylight, they misdirected us to the little town of Horodenka. We drove around the square and a little while later found the right road to Śniatyn.

The day became gray and dreary; the thick, low-lying clouds meant that we were going to get rain soon.

Outside Horodenka, against the background of a large forest, we could see three large tanks, whose insignia we couldn't quite recognize from afar, coming our way. They came to a stop, and we got out of our cars puzzled, frightened to death. We were familiar with German tanks, and knew that we didn't have any. So who did these strange tanks belong to? The roar of their powerful engines became louder as the trio, like planes in a V formation, rapidly advanced on us. We waited in readiness by the ditches so as to protect ourselves against a sudden attack.

"Russians!" someone shouted.

And so they were. We could see the red stars on their grayish brown tanks. We were completely surprised by this and apprehensive about what would happen next. At about 50 meters away the two wing tanks came to a halt in a field with their barrels aimed at us, as if to protect the leading tank that advanced further toward us. It crossed a deep ditch, tearing up rocks with its tread, turned and stopped at the head of our column. The hatch lifted revealing a figure in a helmet who waved in our direction.

"Go on, Stach," Tadeusz said to me. "You know Russian—talk to him. . . ."

I approached the tank with a certain apprehension, but the Russian laughed and wanted me to jump up on the track. His expression didn't indicate any hostile intent, and a little while later I met the leader of their patrol whom I didn't know how to address because I wasn't familiar with Russian insignia. When we shook hands I asked him simply:

"*A wy s nami ili protiw nas?*" ["And are you with us or against us?"]

The Russian smiled broadly and answered:

"Da, s wami! W miestie idiom bit' Giermantsa!" ["Of course, we're with you. Together we're going to beat the Germans!"]

This answer sufficed to transform my apprehension into gladness and enthusiasm.

"They're on our side!" I shouted back to our column, who had been watching our conversation from a distance. We discussed the war situation for a little while, after which the Russian, having bid me farewell, wished us good luck. I jumped off the track as he grabbed the hatch to close it. Smiling, he shook my hand once again.

His engine roared and I could hear him switch gears as the tank moved, made a sharp turn across the ditch, and returned to its comrades. A moment later all three tanks headed back into the forest from which they had come. We watched until they disappeared from view, and then reassured by this immeasurably interesting and important bit of news, went on our way.

Small droplets of drizzle began to appear on our car's window. And the closer we got to Śniatyn, the more the drizzle turned into a heavy rain. As we came upon the town, we could see a burned out Jedenastka not far from the road. Its presence in this area seemed downright incredible. Where did it come from—since all our fighter aircraft remained on the hills surrounding Brzeżany? We stopped to check it out.

"It's my 'Zosia'!" I shouted, seeing the writing on the fuselage. "But how in the world did it get here, and burned out to boot?"

Someone must have made a forced landing in it and it caught fire. This was just another question that we couldn't answer. Who was flying in my plane, and why in this direction?

"Let's go on," said Marian. "Maybe in Śniatyn we'll meet the pilot!"

A half-hour later we were sitting in a tavern in Śniatyn, getting something to eat after spending the entire night on the road, and warming ourselves a bit.

At twelve o'clock the column headed for the border.

When we got outside the town on a hill we saw something strange. Below us the entire length of the road was cluttered with different types of vehicles, crammed together like children's toys. Driving down the hill I watched this enormous procession as I asked myself a new question—the third in the course of the last three hours. Isn't this too much? Where's it going?

The entire queue was backed up to the border-crossing. When we got to the point where the holdup ended, the policeman directing traffic conducted us to a narrow pass between the cars. Military transports had priority. As a result we went to the front of the queue passing by trucks, busses, private and state railways cars, limousines, and taxis from all towns and parts of Poland as if in a subway. At the border-crossing, beside the lowered barricade, high-ranking Polish officers were talking with Romanian authorities who were waiting for the decision of their superiors in Bucharest about opening the border.

There was nothing but bad news everywhere—dark, depressing, shattering news hanging over us with an insurmountable weight. The vision of Hurricanes and Moranes, the vision of continuing the fight, strangely faded. We were faced with the naked truth—the end.

And so this is it? No hope?

We were bewildered.

The orders said that all air force personnel were to escape enemy encirclement and make their way by the shortest route to Romania or Hungary. The orders had reached the units at Brzeżany during the night. In the morning all remaining planes flew to Romania, while the ground crews headed for the border.

At dawn the Soviet army had crossed the eastern border along its entire length, and, advancing, occupied the territory remaining in Polish hands. The tanks that we met at Horodenka were the advance party of the leading armored units. And so the news their commander had given us was not in accord with the course of the developing actions.

The opening of the border-barricade seemed to be the only escape from the situation. But as time passed we became more unruly. We began to hatch crazy plans: not to leave but to stay and hide in the forests and the mountains, and to conduct a guerrilla war against the German invaders.

Indecision paralyzed us. Contradictory ideas swirled in our heads. We told each other all kinds of intentions, but everyone obeyed orders. We were soldiers.

The barricade was raised and the first cars moved across the border. We walked to our trucks, which were somewhere in the rear.

From the low-lying, leaden clouds a heavy rain began to fall. The rain increased, surrounding everything in a dull screen. We exchanged heavy glances with the driver. We were tormented by the same thought!

Our car rumbled, and moved slowly toward the border.

Epilogue

THIS WAS THE BEGINNING OF OUR ODYSSEY—AN ARDUOUS ORDEAL OF battle.

Almost all the fronts of the Second World War were to see Polish airmen. Within a couple of months of the September defeat—right after Göring's solemn guarantees of the complete destruction of the Polish air force—our red-and-white chessboard appeared over France. When after France's defeat threatening clouds hung over England's future, Polish airmen fought with the greatest of skill in the great air battle for its freedom—the battle that history calls the Battle of Britain.

Later, Africa would see them, even the Far East. They flew over oceans—the Atlantic and the Indian.

They showed up everywhere the enemy—Nazi Germany—showed its face, and with courage and skill hastened the hour of its defeat.

The fame of Polish wings enveloped both hemispheres—with our airmen extending it over vast expanses in the West and in the East. Everywhere the engines of our planes sang the old Polish battle song: "*Za wolność Waszą i naszą.*"

Maybe someday I'll write about these years.

Appendix i

POLAND

The Polish air force was in a position to present the following combat aircraft for action:

In the Bomber Force: 4 regiments and 1 squadron (together 9 squadrons), composed of 5 squadrons of 10 Karaś light bombers each and 4 squadrons of 9 Łos medium bombers each, **86 aircraft total.**

In the Fighter Force: 7 regiments and 1 squadron (together 15 squadrons), composed of 12 squadrons of Jedenastka fighter planes each and 3 squadrons of P-7 fighter planes each, **150 aircraft total.**

In the Reconnaissance and Observer Force (line and liaison): 7 squadrons of reconnaissance aircraft of 10 Karaś light bombers and 12 observational squadrons of 7 aircraft each, composed of 8 squadrons of R-XIII aircraft and 4 squadrons of Czaplas, **154 aircraft total.**

Thus taken together, omitting planes of the liaison force, planes of the commanders of line units, in addition to transport planes, the Polish air force was in a position to present 390 aircraft for combat.

(Source—Władisław Żaczkiewicz: *Lotnictwo polskie w kampanii wrześniowej* 1939 r., Warsaw 1947.)

GERMANY

German Luftwaffe Forces on September 1, 1939

30 groups of bombers: including 18 groups of Heinkel He-111 medium bombers, 11 groups of Dornier-17 medium bombers, and 1 group of Junkers Ju-86 medium bombers, 1180 aircraft total.

13 groups of fighter planes: including 12 groups of Messerschmitt Me-109s and 1 group of Arado Ar-68s, 771 aircraft total.

9 groups of divebombers of the Junkers Ju-87 type, 336 aircraft total.

10 groups of the destroyer aircraft of the Messerschmitt Me-109 and Me-110 type, 408 aircraft total.

1 group of attack planes of the Henschel Hs-123 type, 40 aircraft total.

23 squadrons of long-range reconnaissance aircraft of the Dornier Do-17 type, 379 aircraft total.

30 squadrons of short-range reconnaissance aircraft of the Henschel Hs-45, the Heinkel He-46, and Henschel He-126 types, 324 aircraft total.

Naval Aircraft Formations—240 aircraft.

Special units—55 aircraft.

Total: 3,781 combat aircraft.

(Source—G. W. Feuchter: *Geschichte des Luftkrieges*, Bonn 1954.)

Appendix 2

In 1964 in West Germany there appeared a book by Cajus Bekker entitled *Angriffshöhe 4000*, which is a condensed history of the Luftwaffe in the Second World War, based on source material, documents of the inspector general's office, and interviews with Luftwaffe personnel.

It is worth citing the author's opinion in this book about the combat of the Luftwaffe with the Polish air force in September 1939.

The initial attack of the Luftwaffe on Poland on the 1st of September 1939 at 4:45 a.m., before X hour, i.e., before 5:00 a.m., was directed against railway targets between the yard and the bridge in Tczew. The attack of a flight of three Ju-87s did not achieve its intended goal—the saving of the bridge over the Vistula. Polish sappers were able to destroy it.

The German archive and documents became accessible only twenty-five years later. And for us, Poles, what is much more valuable is that the Polish defensive war received detailed consideration.

In his book Bekker cites Luftwaffe losses in this brief war that are greater than those that appear in Polish records. Here are the data from the archive of the inspector general of the Luftwaffe's Office:

285 aircraft destroyed

279 aircraft damaged

734 Luftwaffe personnel lost

And so, in contrast to the Nazi propaganda in 1939, German losses in Poland were considerable.

I would like to cite five points that Bekker draws from the combat in September 1939, and which support the truth concerning the heroic efforts of Polish forces against the Nazi invaders.

The Blitzkrieg against Poland was not a walk in the park, but a difficult struggle against a determined opponent. Considering that the war lasted only four weeks, the Luftwaffe suffered relatively large losses: 734 combatants, 285 aircraft, of which 109 were bombers and divebombers.

Against all expectation, the Polish air force was not destroyed on the ground in the first two days of the war. For example, the bomber brigade was able to attack the German army even on the 16th of September. Giving way both in quality and quantity, Polish aircraft did not permit the Luftwaffe to gain easy air superiority.

Luftwaffe activity in mediate and immediate support of German land forces possessed decisive importance for the rapid course of the campaign in Poland. The destruction of communication centers paralyzed the enemy more than bomber attacks on air bases and industrial centers whose activity was cut short.

Warsaw was not an open city, but a strongly defended opponent. After the fifth call to surrender on the 25th of September, there followed a heavy air attack that compelled the capital to surrender.

The war against Poland was an example of the cooperation of the air force and the land army for subsequent Blitzkriegs. However, experience and results from it demonstrated that the Luftwaffe was strong enough only for a temporally limited warfront.

The evaluation of September 1939 contained in Bekker's book significantly differs from other evaluations encountered in the literature.